How to Save Money & Still Have a Life

by Cristy Johnson

authorHOUSE®

AuthorHouse™
1663 Liberty Drive
Bloomington, IN 47403
www.authorhouse.com
Phone: 1-800-839-8640

First published by AuthorHouse 4/22/2010

ISBN: 978-1-4520-0275-0 (e)
ISBN: 978-1-4520-0273-6 (sc)

Library of Congress Control Number: 2010927274

Printed in the United States of America
Bloomington, Indiana

This book is printed on acid-free paper.

I dedicate this book to Rob, my soul mate, who taught me that it's the memories that last, not the money. I'd be so boring without you!

Table of Contents

Introduction

For the most part, I find introductions boring and I never read them so I'll keep this short.

This book is NOT designed to tell you where to put your savings or which stocks to invest in. It is NOT going to tell you how to make money, like selling your stuff on eBay. And I'm also not going to lecture you on your spending habits. Think of this book, instead, as a way to reroute your money. It's like teaching you how to get from point A to point B via point F – a way to cut some corners so you can buy that scooter or take that vacation. It's about how to save money and still have a life- your life!

Why should you believe me? I have lived in an old apartment, a new apartment, an old house, a new house, a duplex, an end-unit townhome, and a middle unit townhome. I have rented, owned a home, sold a home, and now rent again. I have owned a new car, an old car, and currently make payments on a not-too-new car. I have gone to college, graduated from college, done an internship, and worked my way through it all. I have been single, dated, and am now married with one child, plus one on the way. I have been unemployed, employed, and am now self-employed. I used to never use the internet, then I dabbled, then I pretended to be good, and now I am a self-proclaimed master. I have never come close to making six figures (mega-understatement), but also never wanted to give up my comfortable lifestyle, so I gradually learned to how to shop "correctly." My mother says I can make a dollar stretch farther than anyone else she knows... So you should believe me because I have learned the hard way.

As you read, notice the topics in the first three chapters are arranged in alphabetical order. This was ultimately due to lack of a better way, but in the end makes it easier for you to skip to the parts which you feel are pertinent. The websites mentioned are also in alphabetical order to prevent anyone from thinking I was playing favorites, as I am in no way affiliated with or profiting financially by mentioning their URLs. At the end of the book (Chapter Seven) are charts which should expedite your learning and searching- saving you both time and money. Feel free to dog-ear, highlight, make photocopies of the good pages, then pass this on to someone else who needs it.

Alright, Introduction over!

Chapter One

Getting Started -
Changing Your Perspective

In know in the Intro I said I wouldn't be lecturing you on your spending habits, and I meant it! This section is more about qualities I encourage you cultivate... if you can.

Patience is a Virtue!

First and foremost, you must have patience. If you don't have any to speak of, find some! Most of what this book has to say deals with waiting for shipment, making calls to people who will give you the runaround, filtering through search results, etc. Below I will list some specific examples of key areas to save; if you scoff and say you can't do it, put this book down and go buy something! Without patience, it will be hard to cut any corners.

- When you want something (i.e. a book), try to hold yourself back from buying it immediately. See if you can find the cheapest price on the internet and wait for shipment.

- When you want something large, or you want it now (i.e. a TV), you should go to several stores to compare prices. This includes, perhaps, talking to many different salespeople.
- Rather than buying certain items (i.e. greeting cards), you could take a stab at making them yourself.
- Try to wait for certain items to go on sale (i.e. buy a grill in October instead of May) or for movies to come out on DVD.

If you read that list and thought, "Those are easy!" then you could basically stop reading. While this book has much more meat to it than that, you could start saving immediately just by following those rules. But my point is, if you <u>can't</u> see yourself conforming, then you may just want to choose a better paying job or pick up a second one, rather than focusing on saving money. And I say that with no condescension; I can think of four people I know of, right off the bat, who couldn't possibly do the things I just mentioned!

Get Off Your High Horse!

So many people try to keep up with the Joneses and they're wasting money! Who cares about name brands? Why do you have to have that Coach purse? Okay, that's just my mentality and I certainly know a gazillion people who have to have their name brands (my husband included). So there are two subsections in this section: one geared toward people like me and one geared toward everyone else.

1. If you're like me and don't care about name brands,

then you probably already know where to find the bargains: T.J. Maxx, Ross, Plato's Closet, Goodwill, and other thrift stores. But there are also bargains to be had on eBay (buy in bulk and save!) and Craigslist (people often sell large lots of items in the same sizes). If you can spare the time, visit garage sales on the weekends and you're sure to find some steals. I'm a big fan of clearance racks at Target and Wal-Mart, but you have to be willing to wait to wear the clothes, as those items are usually from the last season, such as t-shirts on clearance in October.

2. If you're in the name brand category, then you probably don't know where the deals are. You could continue to shop at your usual stores, but have a little patience! Visit the clearance racks and know you'll have fun clothes to wear two seasons from now. Or find a Plato's Closet or a store similar (Plato's Closet buys and sells gently used brand name clothing only). You, too, could shop at T.J. Maxx or Ross, and even those thrift stores. You'll just have to make sure you have enough time to sift through the non-name brands. On eBay, you probably won't be able to buy in bulk but you will, most likely, save money.

Sometimes, whether you care about name brands or not, there is just one brand that fits and the rest don't. For example, I'm very short and have a difficult time finding pants, as I still have hips and a butt. So, when I feel up to it, I take a trip to the mall and try on, try on, try on. When I <u>finally</u> find a pair that fits, I write down the brand, the model, and the size. Then, I go home and find it cheaper on the internet (my techniques are in Chapter

Five). But for the most part, I think you could do without your fancy schmancy names. There are plenty of purse imitations, fake diamonds, tasty cheap wine, and knock-off colognes (and 99.9% of the population won't know the difference)! If you're a name brand junkie, maybe take baby steps with this one.

Be Realistic!

In this book, I begin with your *needs*, the things you have to buy and don't have a choice to cut out. This category includes utilities, phone services, food, and other living expenses. Let's be realistic and accept that you have to pay for these things- but let's pay less! So if you're really motivated, you should make a list of all the bills you must pay, no question.

I will then move into the category of wants-that-feel-like-needs. This includes items such as cat litter, vitamins, special dietary needs, personal hygiene, etc. Okay, now you're confused... Yes, my cats *need* cat litter, but I *want* them to use a certain brand. I *need* to eat a certain diet but I *want* to have that great cereal made by so-and-so. Catch my drift? Thinking realistically, I could buy the super cheap cat litter and save money. Or I could eat yo-gurt for breakfast and save money (or not, depending on the yogurt). But I don't *want* to do those things, I want my good cat litter!!! Get it??! So you should make a list of all the items that you could buy cheaper but don't want to. Think laundry detergent, toilet paper, shampoo, pet food, organic produce, etc.

Okay, then I move onto straight wants. You could cook something, but you would rather go out. You don't need another pair of jeans, but you want them. You don't need to spend $100 on your brother's birthday gift, but you want to. Make sense? Make a list of the extracurricular activities, hobbies, and items you *know* you could do without but would rather not.

You see, this book requires that you look at your spending habits and decide, "Do I really need to eat out every other day?" and "Do I really use that many voice minutes a month on my cell phone?" You need to detach yourself from your "things" and determine which changes you can make and which you can't. For those you can, great! For those you can't, (like the name brand face cream you <u>must</u> have), I'll just help you find it cheaper.

Also, as you read, you may see examples or suggestions that will only save you a dollar or two and you might be tempted to think, "What the heck for?" But look at it this way: If you saved five dollars a week, you'd save $260 a year. What could you buy with $260?!

Chapter Two

Attacking Your Required Bills

This chapter discusses the bills everyone has and you don't have a choice to get rid of. Believe it or not, there are some savings to be had! (Topics are listed in alphabetical order...)

Car Expenses

These are definitely needs. If you have a car, you have to buy gas and maintain it. More and more people are deciding to repair, rather than trade-in, their cars due to monetary reasons. Here are just a couple of suggestions for saving money in the motor vehicle department:

- This one you already know about: FuelEconomy.gov, GasBuddy.com, GasPrices.MapQuest.com, GasPrice Watch.com, MotorTrend.com, etc. etc. You can punch in your zip code and the site will tell you which gas station has the lowest prices.
- If you don't have time to look on the internet, just think of the intersection with the most gas stations. More stations means more competition which means lower prices.

- If a certain station consistently has the lowest prices (or comparable), then think about getting one of their gas cards. You'll earn points and/or rebates on your purchases.
- Type "save gas" into your internet search engine. While some of these tips may be legit, there are some which are somewhat dangerous and I, personally, advise against them. Under no circumstances do I think a few dollars are worth putting your safety at risk.
- For maintenance, look on the internet for coupons. I have found the easiest (and maybe only?) place to get these are on the named website themselves, such as ColonyTire.com, GreaseMonkey.com, Jiffy-Lube.com, Meineke.com, and your local oil change service location. Most of them have a link titled "Coupons" or "Specials" which take you to a page you can print.
- These same coupons can also be found for dealerships and repair service shops. It's definitely worth your time to do a quick search on their website. Ten dollars is ten dollars!
- Now might be a good time to learn how to do certain maintenance projects yourself, such as oil changes, brake pad replacement, fluid refills, etc. But this really isn't feasible unless you have the proper tools and someone to hold your hand. Unless you consider that kind of thing "fun," then rest assured you save in so many other areas, this expenditure is okay!
- This is more a warning than anything else! Before you leave the shop, look at your engine and check all your fluids. If one isn't filled (and that was part of your

service) or something looks fishy, don't leave! Talk to a manager. I now boycott two oil change places because I KNOW they messed up my car but of course I have no proof. I now take my car to a dealership because those places have made me distrustful. I pay more, yes, but peace of mind is worth a lot. I'm not saying you should go spend more money on your oil changes, I'm just saying watch your back! (Shout out to Johnson Lexus of Southpoint inserted here- no, I don't own a Lexus! But wish I did...)

- Check your car's air filter- if it's dirty, wash it or replace it. You can check your local auto parts store or even Wal-Mart or the internet. Your car has to work harder to get air through a dirty air filter, plus it's not good for you.

- If you find a store or shop which conducts free diagnostics, amen! Take advantage. Most places charge between $60 and $100 for this service. Another option, of which I don't guarantee the results, is to wait to figure out that "noise" until you have your car in for an oil change. You can ask the person what they think that sound is and you might get a "free" professional opinion. *Disclaimer: I always recommend taking care of funny "noises" right away!

- If your car is doing something funky, look on the internet for recalls. Often, you would have gotten something in the mail but maybe not! If there is a recall for a certain part on your car, dealerships are required to replace it free of charge.

- If you need some minor part (i.e. the hook that holds your visor, the air-pump-thingy that holds your trunk up, a taillight, etc.) check your local junkyard first. The cost will be a fraction of what you'd pay for a new one!

- If you look on CraigsList.com under "Services," you'll find many people willing to make auto repairs and oil changes. I think this is a great resource, I just need to make the recommendation that you go with someone who offers a warranty and that you get all the information you can from such person (address, phone number, a signed receipt with stated warranty, etc.).

Credit Cards

Wow, what a topic. We all have them, I don't care what people say. Knowing that, are we doomed to pay the high interest rates? No.

Okay, let me preface this section because I feel a law suit coming on. I am NOT giving financial advice and I do NOT guarantee the results of your efforts will be successful. There are many criteria involved, such as how much debt you have and how good your credit is. I am not going to get into all that, so by continuing to read, you are entering into a contract with me stating you hold me liable for nothing!

Phew...

I suppose I could have put this Credit Card section into the next one, as you could technically choose to not pay your credit card bill. But, I am assuming you do pay your monthly bill (of which I am a big proponent) so I have kept it here in the Required Bills section. Also, I am humble enough to tell you that at one point in my life, I was putting my rent on credit cards and that the large savings account balance needed to purchase my last house was due to a cash advance (and my mother- shout out!). So I don't care why you have debt. If you decided that having twenty Coach purses was very important, I don't care. What I do care about is you not giving the credit card millionaires more of your hard-earned money. Be prepared, though, to have patience! You are going to have to make phone calls, no internet shortcuts here.

- Get a pad of paper and a writing utensil. Make a list of all the credit cards you have- you can either put them all on their own page or make a neat grid. Under the name of the credit card, put the account number and customer service phone number. (I suggest shredding these sheets when you're finished.) Put the current balance (even if it's zero), your credit limit, and APR. If you don't know these, leave a blank spot for them. Leave spaces for "Balance Transfer Specials" and "Closed?"
- Start calling. Fill in all the blanks except for "Closed?" These are going to be information-gathering calls only! The moment you ask about balance transfer specials, the rep will try to get you to transfer. Hold your ground; either tell them you don't have a balance to transfer or tell them you need to think about it and will call back. They're persistent, these people! And ask what the fees are on those transfers.
- While you have them on the phone, go ahead and ask for a credit line extension. If they ask how much, just say, "The most I can get." You may not use it, but it will save you a step if you do decide to transfer a balance. Also, I *think* it helps your credit (not sure on the specifics). Some can give you an answer right

away, some you have to wait for. Worst-case-scenario, they say no. Big deal.

- Alright, now that your columns are all filled out, you need to analyze. You have a few options:

  1. You could choose the keep the balances where they are, avoiding the balance transfer fees. The way to save money by going this route is by calling them back and telling them you want to close the account. They will pretend that is the saddest thing they've heard all year and will ask why. Your answer should include the words, "My APR is just too high." Most likely (no guarantees from me, remember?) they will offer you a lower APR. If they don't, then you should decide whether you want to be affiliated with a company who doesn't try to keep you as a customer. As a side note, do not try this closing method with an eBay Mastercard- they have a totally automated system and you will not be met with a fight!

  2. You could decide to take advantage of a balance transfer special. You may wonder if the fees make it worthwhile. Good question! There are definitely a couple things to consider. Let's say transferring two balances would cost you $150 ($75 each) and the new APR would be 1% for six months. If you currently pay $10 a month in interest, each, then in six months you would have paid $120, making the balance transfer not worth it. You'll have to look at the numbers, I can't do that for you. Look at your statements to see how much interest you're paying each month. But be realistic- can you really pay off that balance in six months?

3. If you decide you can't pay off the balance in six months but you would really save a lot of money by transferring, then do what I did years ago! Transfer once, then transfer again, then again. Of course, the fees were much lower then and more 0% APR offers were available. Or, research credit cards to find a special giving you an APR for the life of the balance. I have often opened a new credit card because my current ones had nothing to offer in the way of transferring. Here are some great sites for comparing credit cards (in alphabetical order): Bankrate.com, CardHub.com, CardRatings.com, CompareCreditCards.com, CreditCardGuide.com, CreditCards.com, CreditorWeb.com, and many more. I am not affiliated with any of those sites- you can just do what I did and conduct an internet search for "compare credit cards" and choose the site which suits you best!

4. Make sure to read the fine print! Credit card companies have changed their rules lately, it seems. The balance transfer fees are higher and have higher maximums, if any.

5. If you default on a payment for a balance transfer, you will not only be charged a fee but your promotional rate will end and turn into a much higher APR. If this happens, you could try to call the company first to ask for forgiveness (most, it seems, have a first-time-forgiveness policy). If that doesn't work, perhaps consider transferring again? You'll have to crunch numbers!

So good luck with that- expect to spend the better part of your day doing it, too.

If you are a responsible credit card user, I suggest using rewards cards for your purchases. Amazon has its own credit card for which you earn three points for every dollar spent on Amazon.com and fewer points for other purchases. eBay also has its own card, giving you one point for every dollar spent on eBay.com. Of course, there are airline cards and gas cards and other cards. My point is: if you aren't using a rewards card then you're missing out on free money. I just encourage paying off the balance every month so as to avoid the finance charges. Otherwise, that free money isn't so free...

One last thing about credit cards and it's actually something I've never done but have been tempted. I should credit my high school history teacher for the information- he was the sort that could easily be brought off topic and I can't remember his name! Anyway, about the credit cards: if you are the lucky/ responsible sort who has an offer for 0% APR for a given length of time, you could consider writing out one of the checks they send you to a bank to but in a CD or some other savings account. The theory is that when it's all said and done (promotional period ends, CD/ savings time ends) you've actually made money in interest. Granted, it might only be twenty or thirty dollars, but that's twenty or thirty dollars you didn't have before. Of course, you have to plan on making the monthly payments and paying off the balance when the promotion ends. Therein lies the tricky part and where the majority of our population would go wrong. But, I thought I'd throw it out there.

Electricity

I'm not rich so I need to save money on utilities anyway but I'm also all about doing my part to leave a healthy planet for my children. I have replaced all the bulbs in my house with the energy efficient ones (CFLs, or compact fluorescent light bulbs). Yes, some of them can yell at you in the face, but now they make bulbs to mimic the old ones, i.e. vanity and globes. I use some and they're not bad! They do take a little while to warm up but think of all the money you're saving! Besides, it might be nice to not have a light be bright at seven (or six!) in the morning. As for the cost factor: it will definitely take awhile to recoup your money in savings, but I'm certain you'll see a difference in your electricity bill. My last home was on the lowest usage rating for homes of similar size; when I showed my husband, you would have thought I was showing him our child's report card full of A's, I was so proud.

Let's see, more electricity saving ideas...

- Turn off lights when you leave a room. Especially if you're not using the energy efficient ones.
- If you are unwilling to totally convert to CFLs, and have a light or two that you keep on a lot (like your front porch), at least change those.
- Unplug your cell phone chargers when not in use. I know you've heard this, and I know you don't believe it. But, to generalize, any cord with a small black box on it contains a transformer, which constantly sucks a tiny bit of energy from the grid. If you have a phone, and your significant other has a phone, and

your three children have phones, and all the chargers are constantly plugged into the outlets, that's some serious leakage.

- Unplug appliances and other devices when not in use, especially ones with lights or clocks. I have a toaster which has a blue light on it that stays lit, always. I find this annoying, but also know it's draining a bit of energy, all the time, to keep that blue light lit. So I only plug it in when I need to use it. But then there's the coffee maker. It has a clock on it that I rely on while I'm in the kitchen so I do keep that one plugged in. So, you see, I'm not asking you to go unplug your entire kitchen! Just take a step back and prioritize; choose your battles.

- Speaking of the kitchen, turn your refrigerator and freezer temperatures down. I have mine on the lowest settings and can't imagine why people need it colder!

- When you have the oven on to bake a certain item, think of one or two things you could throw in there. For example, wrap some potatoes in foil and bake them, or roast that acorn squash that's been sitting around. It's a small gesture, but if this becomes a habit, those small steps turn into large strides.

- If you cook in small quantities, think of getting a toaster oven. These use a third to half as much energy as a full-sized oven.

- As for the office, turn off your printers!!! I'll say it again, louder this time: TURN OFF YOUR PRINTERS!!! Especially if you have a laser printer... If you aren't running a business and only print once or twice a day, or less, only turn on the printer when you're ready to print and then turn it off when you're done. You see, the drum on the average laser printer stays hot for at least a half hour after the last print, sort of in standby mode. This is an energy hog. You may think I don't know what an inconvenience that would be for you but I do- I have a laser printer hooked up to my wireless network and it is on a different floor than the one where I actually have my computer. So when I want to print, I go upstairs, turn on the printer, go downstairs and print, go upstairs and get the printout, turn off the printer, then go downstairs. Is it inconvenient? Yes. Am I saving money? Yes. This same thought goes for shredders, scanners, copiers, etc. And don't leave your computer running all day- that's a big hog right there. At least put it on standby.

- I'm not sure where to put this but I guess "Electricity" is the best category: invest in rechargeable batteries. Just like windows, it's a cost right at first, but they pay off in the end. I'm the first to admit their juice doesn't last as long as throwaways, but that's not the point. Disposables are poisonous to our landfills, inconvenient to recycle, and expensive. And it's nice to know that I'll never run out of AA's! I'm certain I have recouped my money in a year or two.

- If you won't convert to rechargeable batteries, please recycle your disposables! I believe most hardware stores and Whole Foods grocers have a special bin for them.

Heating and Air Conditioning

I know, I know, you've heard it all before! Lower the thermostat in winter and raise it in summer, blah blah blah. Well, there is actually something to that. At my last place, I could leave the temperature at 67 degrees Fahrenheit in the winter and the furnace would occasionally kick on. But if I upped it to 68 degrees, it seemed like the furnace was running all the time. So I'm convinced each house has it's "threshold", so to speak. I suggest finding out what those thresholds are for your house and changing your habits to conform to those, rather than just letting the furnace or air conditioner run to meet your wants. More suggestions:

- A biggie, in my book, is to make sure your air filters are replaced at regular intervals. They're not that expensive if you buy in bulk and don't have special allergen needs. If your air filters are dirty, then your systems are working harder to get air and are therefore using more energy which costs you money!

- I used to live in Wisconsin and boy, does it get frigid up there! My first December served me up a $170 electricity bill. I lived in a 20 year old apartment with electric baseboard heat and old thin windows. My advice to people in those shoes? Buy one (or two or three) of those kits for sealing up your windows. They're basically cellophane and double sided tape. The less expensive ones aren't pretty and the tape may not come off all the way, but they work!! If you spend a little extra, you can get a kit that is almost crystal clear and you may be able to reuse it the next year.

- Get outlet insulators (little foam pads to put behind the plates) and put them on all non-shared walls. And for the big sliding glass doors? Cover them. Either with the same kind of insulating kits for the windows, a nice curtain rod and thick drapery, or a sheet taped along the edges, whatever suits you. Those things are super drafty!

- Replace your old thermostat with a new programmable one. If your thermostat is ancient, chances are the temperature sensor is not accurate and the toggle switches are annoying. Also, with a programmable one you can, obviously, program it so as to not have your furnace or A/C unit work so hard while you're gone or asleep. It's easier to replace than you think; they should all come with directions and the wires are somewhat universal. You could pay an electrician, and that will run you about $100 (or more!). But your savings will be huge. One website says you could save about 30% on your bills...

- Buy new windows.

WHAT?! You exclaim....

Okay, so that doesn't really save you money. But, here are the perks to new windows:

- ✓ You will see a difference in your monthly heating and cooling bills.
- ✓ You get to brag to all your friends.
- ✓ Previously, you didn't open your windows because the screens are either completely messed up or nonexistent and you didn't want an infestation of bugs. With new windows, you'll have beautiful new screens and no bugs.
- ✓ Because you'll now be able to open your windows (because the old ones were painted shut, which is a fire hazard anyway), you can also heat and/or cool your house with windows and fans during certain months, depending on where you live.

This will give you significant savings on your bill!

✓ Even when you don't have your windows open, your new windows will let in <u>way</u> less heat and cold than your old ones, thus saving you money on your bill.

✓ You can most likely get a tax credit when you file.

✓ When / if you go to resell, new windows are a <u>huge</u> incentive to buy and <u>may</u> get you closer to your asking price. (Please consult with your realtor, don't just take my word for it!)

• Put up nice window blinds and/or curtains. If you leave your windows treatments wide open all the time, STOP! It may not seem like it, but the air trapped between the window and your treatments acts as an insulator against both heat and cold, and that goes for both new and old windows. Plantation blinds are said to be better than aluminum blinds, and roman and cellular shades are supposed to be the best. If you combine blinds with curtains, that's even more effective. Sometimes, this doesn't work for me because I love to have natural light come through. But if the sun is just blaring in, chances are there will still be plenty of light coming through if you close the blinds. At night, especially during the winter, I make sure to close them all.

• If you have a vented gas fireplace, you may have noticed how much cold air blows in during the winter! If you don't use the fireplace, think about sealing it up. I used a black trash bag and painter's tape- not pretty, but effective. You could actually see the bag move in and out.

- Play around with your vents. My current townhouse is three stories with one thermostat on the first floor and one furnace in the attic. If I have all the registers open all the way, the third floor reads 72 degrees and the bottom floor reads 69 degrees. Then the top floor stays warm, but the bottom floor cools off due to the front door and sliding back door. So the heat kicks back on! Unacceptable! So I got some advice from my very knowledgeable dad to "Balance the Registers," based on the fact that air travels the path of least resistance. So I closed one on the third and second floors each (both bathrooms), as well as turning one on each floor halfway closed. Then on the first floor I made sure they were all open full blast. Results? Top floor 68 degrees, bottom floor 69 degrees, with heat kicking on less often. Perfect.

- Try rearranging your rooms. My husband is hot-natured and I am cold-natured. We have arranged our bed so that his side is more under the ceiling fan than mine, and he is also closer to the air vent so the cool air blows on him in the summer. In winter our temp stays down and I just wear sweatshirts...

Insurance

Insurance is similar to credit cards. We all have it (some have more than others) and we all have to pay for it. I know there are exceptions out there but, in my opinion, certain insurances are not optional, hence why I have put them in the "Needs" chapter.

For car, renter's, homeowner's, and life insurance,

you're simply going to have to get quotes and compare rates. I said "simply," that's funny. There's nothing simple about it. If you're determined to pay the least amount, you will talk to at least five companies in each area. Here are a couple of suggestions to help you out:

- Know the coverage you want before you make the calls or emails. Otherwise, you're going to have chicken scratch on tiny pieces of paper with numbers all over the place. If you're happy with the numbers you have now, I'd just use those as a guideline to see who's offering the lowest rates. Once you decide that, then you can negotiate terms with that one company.
- Don't email or go through websites for quotes. I am definitely an ATM, self-checkout, buy online kind of person. My husband is more a go to the teller, go through a checker, buy from a salesperson kind of person. Hey, it takes all kinds! But, when it came to car insurance, I tried to get quotes from a bunch of companies online and you know what happened? They all came back with emails saying, "We got your request! Give us a call at such-and-such a number for your quote!" That's when my husband got the task handed to him. So if you want to save yourself some time and energy, go straight to the source via phone. And save yourself some SPAM, too.
- You'll be tempted to go with Company C before you've checked out Company D, E, or F because you like the agent for C. Don't do this! Do your pocket-book a favor and check out all the companies on your list before choosing one.
- If your employer sends you some information say-

ing you get a discount by going with Mr. Insurance (I made that name up), don't buy it! Mr. Insurance could very well be the cheapest one for you, but I wouldn't take anyone's word for it, especially not my employer who most likely has a financial interest with that company. I say this from experience, too. Total sucker.

- I think there's a database of some sort that companies can look at when they're talking to you. My husband said, when I made him call around, that they seemed to know what he was already paying and what his coverage was. *If* this is true (I'm not accusing), use it to your advantage to negotiate.

- Don't be loyal. Okay, you can if you want to, that's your prerogative. I had a 94 year old lady tell me her husband stuck with the same insurance company for some crazy amount of years because he trusted them. I totally get how that was important back in the day, but I don't think that really counts for much now. You decide. I have had three car insurance companies in three years. There's always a better deal to be had!!

- If you decide you want to be loyal, try calling your current company to fake-cancel. They'll ask why and you'll say they're just too costly. See what happens.... Be prepared to be signing up with another company in case they believe you, though!

Okay, for health insurance: I'm pretty much not going to say anything. Too many ifs, ands, and buts in that topic. I'm scared of "pre-existing conditions" and the other ridiculous rules so I have just stuck with the same company for about five years. Sorry I can't/won't help you there.

Phones

To have a landline or not to have a landline? That is the question.... that only you can answer. I had one, then I didn't, then I did, and now I don't. I am old enough to remember when landlines were the only option and this section would be telling you how to compare long distance companies. But, alas, we are in not in the eighties anymore! I honestly don't see the point in having a landline EXCEPT as a number to give companies such as credit cards and catalogs you order from. Then it would become a phone you never answer. I'm sure there are all sorts of other reasons to have a landline so I'm not saying get rid of it; just maybe analyze and figure out why you have one and if your reasons are valid. If you decide to have one, then you have to figure out who has the best deals. You could have a real telephone line, or have a cable phone line. In my experience, the bundled services (where you combine your cable, internet, and phone into one bill) are not the most cost effective. Of course, that may depend on how much you use the phone... I barely used mine and here's what I found:

- Advertised rates are not the lowest rates. Ask the representative what the lowest rate is (be blunt with this question) and they have to tell you. I found a rate that gave me 100 minutes a month for $9.99- the cable company couldn't compete with that.
- Ask for a fixed rate. If you don't, or there isn't one available, expect to see your monthly bill slowly rise.

This happened to me and I called to complain; I was switched to a fixed rate.

- Beware of the contract you entered! I tried to cancel mine early, of course forgetting I had signed a two-year contract. I was informed that I would have to pay a $150 early cancellation fee! Well, I had two months left so it was just more cost-effective to wait out the contract, then cancel.

- Negotiate, negotiate, negotiate! I was told by a certain someone named Bruce that, "There is always room for negotiation." This negotiation could take many forms: threatening to cancel, complaining, asking nicely, price-matching, or the traditional price-haggling. You'll find a strategy that works best for you!

Cell phones! Now, there's a topic! A month ago, my two-year contract was up so I was excited to shop around for phones and plan prices. That excitement quickly drained and it turned into a month-long process. For six years I stayed with the same company because it was easier. Trust me, I won't blame you if you do the same! But if you decide to ride the Change Horse, read these suggestions first:

- Shop through a rebate site if you can (read Chapter Five).
- Shop with a site like LetsTalk.com or Wirefly.com. These sites are great at lining up companies, phones, and plans side-by-side. I bought my last phone through one of these (and my rebate site) and received $35 cash-back!
- Most companies have similar rates and plans, more or less. So it's really the fine print you have to read.

Research perks like coverage, rollover minutes, mobile-to-mobile calling, number of free calls (like friends and family members), etc. You may want to write it down on a piece of paper with columns and the like.

- Have an idea of your average minutes usage. Being charged for overage is a pain!

- Be realistic. Back in the day, I tried to get my husband to go without texting because we didn't want to pay for it. Yeah, the next bill was $30 *more* because he couldn't keep his thumbs still. So we bit the bullet and bought the cheapest plan ($4.99 for 200 texts).

- Watch out for those pictures! Luckily, our current messaging plan includes pictures, but if yours is a text-only plan, those pictures can get pretty pricey!

- The really fancy phones have higher plan rates, I think because they require internet time. So I know you want the latest Blackberry or iPhone, but if you're really strapped for cash, you should ask yourself whether you *need* the latest Blackberry or iPhone. If yes, fine- just shop around! If no, then you just saved yourself a bunch of money.

- Read phone reviews before you decide on one. I originally thought a touch screen phone would be cool but then I read a bunch of reviews saying that this one particular phone kept freezing up. I would hate to have spent my precious money on that phone! Learn from other people's "mistakes" by reading reviews first!

- When you finally have your phone, you'll want to start downloading games and ringtones. Wait! I won't talk about the games, as you'll just have to decide how badly you want that game. But I can speak to the ringtones... I made my own! For my current phone, the company wanted $4.49 per ringtone. No way, José! Instead, I chose a song from my computer, trimmed it using a sound editing program (there are free ones on the internet for download- many give you a free trial period), emailed it to my phone, then set the "sound" as my ringtone. It's not as sharp or loud as the purchased kind, but I now have several songs that I would have paid over $25 for. That's gas money! Well, almost.

Water

Did you know that Americans use over twice as much water as Europeans? We use something like 150 gallons per person per day (different internet sources have different numbers, but I'm close). That's a lot of water!!! Here are some ways to save on your water bill:

- Put bricks in your toilet tank. You probably don't have enough money or time to buy the nice dual flush toilets, but for less than a dollar a pop, you could buy some bricks at your local hardware store. I'm not a brick specialist so I'm not clear on the rust issue. To be safe, I wrapped the bricks in freezer bags and made sure they didn't leak. Then I put them in the toilet tank and played around with the water level. It may take a week or two to figure out the lowest setting for proper flushing, but I think it's worth it.
- If it's yellow, let it mellow. If it's brown, flush it down. In my household, we flush our toilets about every third, sometimes fourth, flush. And of course,

"brown" gets flushed immediately. This can be quite surprising to guests, and we try to remember to check the toilets before they come over. At 1.6 gallons per flush, the savings can add up quickly. Let's say you live alone and you only combine two urinations with others in a day. That's about 96 gallons a month! If you and your significant other both do that, it's more like 192 gallons a month. Even if you don't do it for the money, you should do it for the environment!

- Buy a low-flow showerhead. I have a basic one which I bought for under ten dollars. It puts out only 1.5 gallons per minute, while the average showerhead pours a hefty four gallons per minute. There are several websites which will figure the cost savings for you, but you get the gist. The low-flow head takes a little getting used to (I have to use less conditioner- hey, that saves money, too) but you're saving some water for the whales (and your children).

- I would say hand wash your dishes and that would save you money, but I'll admit I'm addicted to my dishwasher. If you're like me, here're a few things you could do:

  1. Run the dishwasher at night. Many utility companies have different rates for usage at different times of day, with nighttime being the "cheapest."

  2. Make sure it's full. The more you can play Tetris (without blocking the little head that goes up to the top), the more efficient your water usage.

  3. Use the "Light" cycle and don't heat dry. If you rinse your dishes before putting them in and don't mind a little water while pulling them out,

then you'll save a significant amount of water and energy!

- I'm lucky enough to have a high efficiency clothes washer but I could spout off a bunch of people who don't. You could follow the same principles as the dishwasher: run it at night and wash full loads. Also, use cold water when you can.

- Turn the temperature down on the hot water heater tank. You'll get a lot of different answers on this one, all ranging from 110 degrees to 140. From what I gather, 140 is the ultimate max, while 120 is needed to make sure all bacteria is killed. You should talk to someone with more professional knowledge than me, but it's definitely worth looking into.

- Please, please, please, do not run the sink water while you brush your teeth or shave. If you make no other changes, just do this one! If you continue to run the water, you aren't even trying!

- Learn proper watering techniques for your garden. Many plants do better with bi-weekly deep watering, rather than daily light watering. So just do a little research on your specific plants and try to coordinate your watering times to non-evaporative times of day.

- If you have the initial money to invest and the space to accommodate them, check into rain barrels. You'll be amazed at how much water they collect! Many have hose attachments and screens to keep mosquitoes and debris out. If you can use free water to feed your garden, why not? Plus, the plants won't get all the chemicals... There are SO many to sources to purchase from but one of my favorites is the stylish stackable kind from CleanAirGardening.com.

- If you're super gung-ho about saving water, there are many resources out there, especially from California and other western states. Suggestions include collecting your waiting-for-the-water-to-get-warm water in buckets to water your plants and switching to zero landscaping.

Chapter Three

Approaching Your Wants-
That-Feel-Like-Needs

We buy a lot of things that we can't do without, like deodorant and soap, but we spend extra money on certain brands of those items. So I won't be telling you to not bathe (I think I'd have to change the subtitle of this book) but I'll be helping you to bathe on a budget without compromising your brands.

First I need to mention the methods of saving in this area, as you may not be able to do one or any of them!

- Do you have the storage to buy in bulk? If they're needs, chances are they're consumable needs and you'll go through the bulk you have, so if you have the room it's a great idea. For example, you'll eventually go through twenty rolls of toilet paper (a consumable need) but not black Mary Jane shoes (not a consumable need). I used to live in a 500 square foot apartment and there was no way I could have bought in bulk. If you don't have the room, you don't have the room.

- Do you have the money to buy in bulk? Buying in

bulk takes a sizeable amount at first. Yes, you'll be saving money, but you won't feel it right away. You'll feel it in about two weeks when you're at the store and you think, "No, I actually don't need shampoo!" and your checkout total is less than normal.

- Do you have time to shop around? Different stores have different prices on different items. If you are gung-ho about getting the best prices, you can sub-scribe to online flyers from your local grocery and general merchandise stores to browse their sales. Then you can make a list of what you'll get where. If you can buy and store in bulk, this may very well be worth your time.

- Do you have time to clip coupons? There is no real easy way about clipping coupons, in my opinion. You have to look for the ones you'll use then actually clip them and keep them organized. When used correctly (read next bullet) there are some real savings to be had, especially if your store offers double or triple coupons and/or accepts competitor coupons.

- Beware of coupons! Let's say you clip a coupon for a name brand cereal. Ordinarily, you buy the ge-neric store brand but figure you now have a coupon! Crunch the numbers; if the "good" cereal with the coupon still costs more than the store brand, then don't use it! So many people use coupons just because they have them; they wouldn't have bought the prod-uct if they didn't. I say only use a coupon if it's an item you already buy on a regular basis!

- Do you have the patience to shop at certain stores or to shop around? This is probably the biggest question of them all! My example refers to Wal-Mart; we all know Wal-Mart has great prices and there are lots of them (and they sell everything under the sun). But we also know they are all busy and packed, especially on the weekends. You will save money by shopping there, but you must have patience to do so. You could try shopping there during the week and in the mornings, but if you have a regular nine to five job that may not be possible. So I guess my only real advice is to make a list before you go, saving you multiple trips. The other half of this part refers to possibly shopping at multiple stores to get your deals (like the local "dollar" store if you don't care about brands and the big hardware stores for the industrial-sized cleaning supplies). On the plus side, if you buy in bulk you'll rarely have to muster up the saintly quality of patience!

Okay, now on to WHERE to save on these items!

Cleaning Supplies

In general, cleaning supplies fall into the same category as pet food in the sense that their weight makes for a high shipping cost. One exception to that is if you use some obscure or natural product that is very expensive or simply not carried by your local stores. You could try Drugstore.com, MrsMeyers.com, PlanetNatural.com, SeventhGeneration.com, or Vitacost.com. If you're a clean-a-holic and/or you have the storage space, then you might check out websites geared toward "janitorial" supplies to get a wholesale, bulk discount.

As for just buying them normally, every once in a while at the store, I personally don't think it's worth my time to drive to a certain store to save fifty cents on one item. So, I take the time to make a list of all the items I might need in the next two months and *then* go to that special store. What is that special store? Well, for me, it's Wal-Mart (on a Tuesday or Wednesday, probably) but just the other day I went to Target because they sent me a pack of coupons for their Up & Up brand. I used them all and saved a bundle, even though I now have three boxes of dishwasher detergent. I need to give a toilet paper shout-out here: Call me crazy, but I have for several years bought the more expensive toilet paper because I thought it was worth it. I have tried just about every generic brand and figured I spent the same when I used three times as much of the generic stuff per potty visit. UNTIL! I decided to try Target's Up & Up brand toilet paper because I had a coupon and I had never tried it (I'm open-minded!). Of course you'll have to decide for yourself, but I love it because it is definitely comparable and much cheaper. Okay, continuing on... A list and one trip every couple months or so, preferably with coupons, are where the savings are at.

If you don't feel the need to stock up on general merchandise supplies or aren't a list-making person, then I advise you to just buy it along with your groceries and justify it with the fact that you save in so many other areas. Your time is much too valuable to be spent saving less than one dollar on one item you're only going to buy every three or four months, if that.

Food – Traditional or "Normal"

Ah, food. An annoying necessity. I often think of how much money I could save if I didn't have to eat and how much I could get done if I didn't have to sleep. But I have come to terms with these inevitabilities. There are several different types of food shoppers out there:

1. The single mother of two who has to watch every penny and can't buy extravagant items
2. The young couple who eats out more frequently than in
3. The older couple who enjoys cooking together
4. The small family who is somewhat financially secure but can't splurge unnecessarily
5. The large family who has no choice but to buy large quantities
6. The well-established woman who can buy what she pleases
7. The bachelor who buys what he feels like at the moment
8. Etcetera etcetera etcetera

I'm sure I didn't list your "type" but know that I understand no one can have the same buying habits. So, I will assume that you know what's best for your family and will only try to give vague advice which can pertain to multiple types of shoppers.

• Buy a chest freezer. Maybe you don't have the money, or maybe you don't have the space. I fell into both those categories for a long time. But now I have a small one in my hallway closet! It is SO nice to see a great deal in the store and not have to pass it by simply because I don't have the space.
• If you aren't loyal to a certain store and have many local grocers to choose from, try perusing the flyers

first to see which store has more sales on the items you need this trip.

- If you consume meat, look for meat that is almost past its date and you might find savings. My local grocer puts "$2.50 off" stickers on meat they need to phase out; I figure I'm going to freeze it anyway so what the heck. Even if you don't need meat this trip, and can afford it and have the freezer space, buy it anyway as it'll save you money later!

- Also if you consume meat, but not very much, still check into buying large packs as it's often cheaper this way. Then, when you get home, put single-serving sizes into freezer bags. If you remember, write the contents and date on them.

- If you only need canned or boxed goods and aren't concerned with brands, try a store like Big Lots or your closest dollar store. They often have a non-perishable foods section where you can find substantial savings!

- If you only need the basics, nothing crazy, then check out Aldi. I went there for the first time several months ago and was quite impressed. Yeah, there are off-the-wall names but bananas are bananas, in my book. Just make sure to bring your own bags or boxes! There are only a handful of Aldi's, though, which is the only reason I don't go there more often (it's a twenty minute drive one way).

- Give store brands a shot! I'll be the first to admit that name brands are, in general, of better quality. But I would rather save money than worry about the extra amount of crumbled chips in the chip bag. Sometimes, you might not think it's worth it, and that's okay! I'll give you two personal examples: 1) A certain store brand of mustard has a bottle that stays squeezed in when you get to the last of it. Drives me crazy, and I won't buy it anymore. 2) A certain store brand (different store than #1) had canned French-cut green beans for a super low price. I bought several and discovered there were twig fragments included! Maybe it was just that batch (hence the price?) but I'll never buy that brand of green beans again! The important thing is, though, that I tried them. There are countless items that are great, some that my husband even likes *more* than the name brands! That says something!

- If you are brand-conscious and have storage space, Sam's Club is for you! I had a membership once and used it significantly. After a while, though, I decided I would save more money by shopping store brands. Your call... depends on what you buy, I think.

- Did you know that you can freeze milk? Now that my son drinks some twenty to thirty ounces of whole milk a day (and pees that much, too) I find this a huge plus! Milk is expensive, I know, and when you see a special you want to jump on it! If you do, just remember to empty out a little from each container first and set it upright, not on its side or else the container will change shape and you'll have an interesting thaw period. I have found that 48 hours in the refrigerator to thaw works best (for a gallon). Ask your local store if they have case specials; I know Whole Foods gives ten percent off of each case (four gallons)!

- Check into freezing other items, as well, especially seasonal items that are only on sale during certain times of the year. I know that cantaloupe and other melons, if cut up, freeze and thaw nicely, as do cooked carrots, beets, and potatoes. If you can buy your produce in season and save them for later, you'll save!

- If you like winter squashes (acorn, spaghetti, butternut, etc.) and see them for a good price, buy them! The same goes for potatoes, in my book. These foods keep for a long time and are one of those things that you can throw in the oven when you're already cooking something (saving electricity, as I mentioned in Chapter Two).

Food - Organic and Special Diets

I separated this topic from "Food" in general because I think it takes a whole different set of shopping skills.

- If you want to eat organic but can't fathom the prices, try picking and choosing. Type "which foods to eat organic" into your internet search engine and you'll find lists of foods that have more reason to be organic than others. Such foods include peaches, strawberries, lettuce, potatoes, and milk.
- If there's a certain brand that you prefer, check out their website for coupons. Sometimes, you can subscribe to their mailings which include coupons, or sometimes there are coupons you can print from the website itself.
- As a rule, organic items are more expensive in traditional grocery stores than in a store like Whole Foods, Trader Joes, or the local Farmer's Market. So if you plan to buy many organic items, it may be worth your time to shop at one of those places.

- I must tell you that many produce items at Farmer's Markets are not actually organic. I have asked many producers and they have told me they do, in fact, use pesticides. But there are three reasons why shopping with them is still a good idea!
  1. You're supporting your local farmers! Always a bonus!
  2. The food has a less distance to travel, thus cutting the *amount* of pesticides used.
  3. The food has a less distance to travel, thus cutting down the price.
- Many meat and dairy items at Farmer's Markets are indeed organic but you should ask first if it is important to you.
- Buying produce items that are in season, as mentioned previously, is still a good way to buy an item at a lower price.
- If you would like to buy items that are non-perishable (and sometimes perishable!) then check out the internet. I buy six bags of cereal and six loaves of bread (each considered a "case") at a time from Amazon.com. For the cereal, the price is much cheaper than buying it individually at the store and for the bread, I simply can't find that particular one in the stores. There are also certain grocery items on eBay.com, and you could check out the website of those particular items, as you can often order straight from the maker.
- If you aren't into flyers or mailings, specialty food stores should maybe be your exception. If you do your main grocery shopping at traditional grocers, but would like to buy organic every now and then, check out the mailings for sales. When you see one

that piques your interest, you might then make the trek and stock up on that item. My example is a sale Whole Foods occasionally has on their ground beef. When I see that it's $2.99 a pound, I buy a LOT!

- If you have decided that organic items at traditional grocery stores are just too expensive and therefore quit visiting the "natural" section, try again! Just walk by, every time. You see, these items don't move as quickly so every once in a while, the store puts a really good sale or clearance on to clear out a batch. It's worth a shot; worst case scenario is you don't buy anything. Best case, you find a steal!

Personal Hygiene Products

Think lotion, shampoo, soap, toothpaste, etc. I personally do not enjoy shopping for these items and therefore usually buy the same brands and lots of them. So I have looked into buying them in bulk on the internet and can give some generic advice: if the item is under ten dollars or more than ten pounds, you might as well just buy it in the store. Buying relatively cheap items online will not generate a substantial savings as the shipping cost usually makes up for the difference in price. Then if you find a website that has great shipping rates, the items are actually *more* expensive than in the stores (I won't name any names for fear of lawsuits!). So, since time is money, just look for specials at your local store and stock up if you can.

Alright, now think of items that are more than ten dollars. Razor blade refills, cologne and perfume, wrinkle cream, and the like. Definitely, definitely, buy these things online! First, have an idea of what it retails for in the store.

Then check out Amazon.com, Drugstore.com, eBay.com, HealthWarehouse.com, or LuckyVitamin.com. You could even try the websites for the stores you shop at as they might have online specials or promotional codes: CVS.com, Kohls.com, Overstock.com, RiteAid.com, Target.com, Walgreens.com, Walmart.com, etc. For more obscure and/or natural products, try Avon.com, Puritan.com, QVC.com, ShopNBC.com, SkinStore.com, Vitacost.com, VitaminShoppe.com, etc. I'm sure I've missed about fifty sites. This first purchase may take awhile as you search multiple sites but after that one, you'll then know which site to go to straight away! It's definitely worth it. Before you start, though, read Chapter Five to learn the best way to internet shop (I tell you how to find and use promotional codes, get rebates, how to search, etc.).

I should mention something that will save you loads and that is you should be open to used or open-box items. Now, I'm not talking about deodorant or toothbrushes- I'm specifically talking about perfume, cologne, and razor blades. These items cost a fortune! I find it ridiculous, actually, but I need to shave... My mother likes this Christian Dior perfume and wanted more for Christmas one year. I went on eBay, found a bottle that had about an ounce gone, no packaging, and I saved about fifty dollars! No joke. For my husband's cologne, I use eBay and find bottles that were testers. If you feel weird about it, just wipe the whole thing down with disinfectant when you get it. As a side note, be certain of the size you want; if you're not careful, you'll end up with one of those tiny little sample bottles. For our razor blades, I find them in large quantities (thirty or more) and usually they are either loose or in packaging of a foreign language. Who cares??! If you do, I won't criticize, but you'll definitely not be taking advantage of these savings. So the two sites I recommend for these, in particular, are eBay.com and Craigslist.com (lots of people don't want to mess with eBay). Before venturing, check out Chapter Six where I give some pointers on shopping with eBay.

Pet Products

When it comes to pet food and cat litter, you can reasonably assume that buying online will actually cost you *more* money due to shipping fees. Of course, there will be exceptions, I'm sure. Your best bet for saving on these items is to clip coupons or subscribe to mailings which will notify you of sales and/or give you coupons. You could also visit eBay.com and bid on coupons (you'd be amazed at how many coupons you can buy from that auction site!).

PetCo has a program where if you buy ten bags of the same food (same brand and size) then you get the eleventh free. Both PetCo and Petsmart have a savings card which is free. I'm not as familiar with any other large pet food chains, but I know that Target and Wal-Mart have reasonable prices on pet products. As for grocery stores, I think that's hard to say as they carry a limited brand selection. My general thought is they are more expensive. You probably already know which store carries your food of choice at the best price. Unless your pet's food is very specialized, it may be worth your time to shop around.

When it comes to smaller pet items (supplements, treats, toys, etc.), I'd be willing to put money on you saving via the internet. For example, I paid $8.29 at a local store for Greenies Pill Pockets for one of my cats. I knew I could find it cheaper on the internet but I needed it right then! When it came time for a refill, I went to the web and found the same product for $6.99. Big deal, you say! Well, I had a promotional code for $5 off my order, I got free shipping, and a 6% rebate. Did I save? You betcha!

As for prescription items, don't assume all items are prescriptions! I made this mistake; I bought a milk protein supplement for my cat for over a year before I realized it was an over-the-counter item! I still kick myself... If your item is a supplement and not a prescription, try one of these websites: 1800PetMeds.com, Amazon.com, DrsFosterSmith.com, eBay.com, EntirelyPets.com, Medi-Vet.com, PetCo.com, Petsmart.com, and many others! If you actually have prescriptions and are trying to save money, here's something to consider and ask around: when I tried to purchase a feline heartworm prevention medicine from an online dealer, I was sent a letter from my vet claiming that the online dealers do not follow strict rules for shipping and storage of such items (for example, they might be kept in a hot, metal storage locker rather than the climate-controlled veterinarian office). I'm not going to presume to know the accuracy of such claims- I just needed to mention it to you so you can make the best decision for yourself and your pets.

Chapter Four

Addressing Your Wants

Okay, so when I say "Wants" I'm talking about everything else. They're the things that would be first to go if something tragic were to happen financially, like the annual vacation or lavish Christmas presents. They're also the things to decrease in frequency if you got too busy, like going out to eat or watching movies. Included, as well, are items which you can wait to purchase, like a new bedroom suite or flat-screen TV.

Books and Textbbooks

I'm pretty sure that I don't have the power to put the large bookstores out of business (nor do I want to!) so I will admit that I have not purchased a book from a physical store in about three years. I have been to one, though, many times. I go and browse, then write down the ISBN numbers of the books I want, then go home and find them online for much cheaper. If you're like me and don't care if the item is marked up with a fold in the cover, then you stand to save a great deal! And if you're like my brother and can't stand to have even one dog ear or highlight, then you'll still save, just not as much.

- You already know about Amazon.com, but you should also try AbeBooks.com, Alibris.com, Biblio.com, BookCloseouts.com, BookFinder.com, DiscountNew AndUsedBooks.com, eBay.com, Half.com, or just type the ISBN into your search bar. Patience...

- You should never pay full price for a textbook! I realize you sometimes don't have an option (like a new publication) but often you do. You will pay a fraction of the price by shopping online. Just make sure you have, absolutely, the correct ISBN. If you can't find the ISBN (because the website for your college bookstore is sneaky) then check every detail you have, such as edition, author, and the cover illustration. Try this trick my husband discovered: right click on the picture of the book and act like you're going to save it. When you get to the screen where your computer asks you what you want to name it and where you want to put it, you'll see what the listing creator saved it as originally and often it is the ISBN! No guarantees but it's worth a shot. Amazon.com, BigWords.com, CampusBooks.com, CheapestText-books.com, eBay.com, eCampus.com, Half.com, Textbooks.com, or try typing the ISBN into your search bar.

- Something I just came across and tried out is Chegg.com, which is actually textbook rental. When you're done with the book, you send it back, and shipping is inclusive in the price of the rental. Plus, they plant a tree for every rental or sale. We saved a bundle!

- If you love to read but aren't into collecting bookshelf fillers, then you probably already have three library memberships. Why don't more people borrow from the library, I wonder? The membership is free if you're a resident, and the borrow period is 21 days with five renewals per book (at my county library, see yours for details). I suppose when people think "library" they envision the tedious task of going to the building, searching for a book, standing in line, then forgetting to return the book only to be charged for it. Well! Many libraries have online reserve systems where you can, from your comfortable couch, special order the book you want and you will be notified when it is ready. Also, online under "My Account" you can view your book borrowing history. Seriously, check it out!

Candles, Picture Frames, Trinkets, etc.

This is a tricky subject. Some people love little knick knacks and other people can't stand chotchkies (definition: worthless piece of home decor). I fall into the latter category but I respect the views of those who do not consider such things as clutter.

- If your figurines are dear to your heart, then I resign myself to say that those are the reason you save your money elsewhere. Shopping for such items on the internet can be very difficult and time consuming and, from what I understand, most were either gifts or simply called out to you at a store.
- If you do not appreciate things that require a shelf which you must dust later, then you're saving money already! For the ones you already own, consider donating them and receiving a tax write-off or giving

them as white elephant gifts (thus saving money). Make a point to ask for "no knick knacks" for your birthday or the holidays; that way, you'll get gifts you actually like.

- Moving past trinkets... as I am totally biased and it is coming out on paper...

- If you like candles just to have candles, then check out the dollar store! They usually have loads of smaller candles as well as candle holders and the quality is not bad at all!

- If you like certain name brand candles, I have found that the best time to buy is after the seasons have changed. For example, shop in January for a great deal on holiday-scented ones.

- I think a great holiday gift is a picture frame, either filled with a picture of your family or empty. Throughout the year, I browse stores for picture frames on clearance and every once in awhile I find a bargain! I then stock up on them and stash them in a closet until Christmas time. I'm not the type of person who is done with their holiday shopping by July, but I think picture frames are harmless and useful!

Clothing & Shoes

In Chapter One, I hinted at some of the ways to save on clothes, mostly regarding brand name clothing. I'll go over those again, but there are way more hints to be given!

- Fun places to shop are discount clothing stores like T.J. Maxx, Ross, and Marshalls. There may be a few smaller-name stores near you, but those are the big three. From what I understand, they buy the excess merchandise the other big stores didn't buy, then they sell it for less. So usually, the items are all "in style" and from big names. And they don't just sell clothes! Shoes, jewelry, home goods, you name it!

- Second hand stores are a big favorite of mine. Plato's Closet is a name you may have heard of; they buy gently used, name brand clothing then resell it. When I have shopped there, the items have all been of great quality and nicely organized, versus some of the other second hand stores that take hours to sift through. Goodwill is another name I *know* you've heard of but maybe never visited. At my local Goodwill, the clothing is organized by article (i.e. pants, shirts, dresses) then arranged by color. They are not arranged by size. While there will be some items you know have been there for years, you will also come across some treasures, from Ralph Lauren to Old Navy. And many of the items are in great shape, I must say! I do think their staff goes through the donated items and weeds out the un-sellables, but that is just my assumption. If you have never gone there, I implore you to give it a shot! You'll also be helping your community by doing so. For other places to shop, I bet you have a bunch in your nearest big city. Do an internet search for "consignment" and type in your city's name. When I did this for my city, I came up with about ten shops within local driving distance. I think shopping at consignment stores is especially important for children's clothing- they grow out of them too fast to spend an arm and a leg!

Plus, because they grow out of them so fast, the items are often in like-new condition.

- Clearance racks, clearance racks, clearance racks. If my husband can't find me in a store (because I'm short and I forgot my phone), he goes for the clearance racks. I don't care which store we're talking about, just visit those first. Sure, you may be looking at t-shirts in January, but you'll be wearing those before you know it! I was just at a favorite store of mine and they had boys' short-sleeved shirts for one dollar! Right now, it's too cold so I just bought the next size up and we're ready for summer. To shop effectively at clearance racks, you just need to think ahead and be willing to wait to wear the new items. Often you may not find anything in your size or style, but sometimes you'll find a steal; it's worth passing by every time.

- Target and Wal-Mart actually have really cute clothes. Those two stores try to keep up with the latest trends and have very competitive prices. You may not think of those two names when you think "clothing," but you should!

- Kohl's. I need to do a shout out here: "KOHL'S!" If you have not discovered the amazing qualities of Kohl's, you are missing out, let me tell you. They *always* have sales, always. So if you want a shirt that you can wear tomorrow, and you want it for a great price, go to Kohl's. I often get "extra" savings in the mail, little cards you take with you that give an extra 15%, 20%, or even 30% off. If you don't get those in your mailbox, try signing up for their mailings by visiting Kohls.com. Their website is also great for clothes you don't need to try on. Think men's work clothes, children's clothes, socks, etc. Sometimes, shipping is free if you spend a certain amount and you can still use those cards you got in the mail. Or, you can find a coupon code from the internet to get the same percentage. Then, if you shop through a rebate site (check out Chapter Five for tips on how to shop on the internet) you may get something like 3% cashback (depending on the site). If you see a great deal on something you'd rather try on, you could order it anyway, as you can just return the items to a Kohl's store (bring the receipt mailed with your items). I could write a whole chapter on Kohl's, I think.

- There are a lot of internet sites for awesome-priced clothing. I won't list any, as there are way too many and the ones I don't mention will get mad, I'm sure. So just type the article of clothing you want (example: "women's jeans") into your search engine and you'll get a slew of results. As a precaution, I suggest knowing the measurements of the person you're shopping for, as we all know every store has a different set of sizing rules, it seems. Most clothing websites have a sizing guide for their items so you can cross-check. Also, be realistic. If you're short, like me, expect that the lengths of the pants and sleeves will be a little long, unless you can order petite size. Same goes for the tall people out there. If you can sew, or are willing to try, or have a gracious friend or mother, then you can be more daring as there's the option to hem. One drawback to think about is that you can't return the items to a storefront and if you do return an item via mail, your shipping fees usually aren't refunded. But,

I have found that the prices on these sites are so great I don't mind one or two items that don't fit right.

- One time I went to a nice store in the mall to find dress pants. I found the perfect ones! But then I got sticker-shocked. I resolved to find them cheaper on the internet. I wrote down the brand, the size, the "model" (by that I mean slim, boot cut, straight leg, etc.), and the price and went home. Plug the brand name and article (like, "Joe pants") into the search bar and see what you get. Then visit the sites, search for your size and model, and compare prices. Then factor in shipping cost.

- Where did I ultimately buy those pants? Ebay. Yep, and they were brand new! And I got a cash-back rebate by going through a rebate site. So when you're checking out the internet for those brand names, don't forget about eBay.com or some other auction site of your choice. Read Chapter Six for tips on how to successfully shop on eBay.com.

- Craigslist.com is another avenue to venture on for clothes. I imagine 99.9% of these items are used, as that's really what the site is mostly about. What I recommend searching for are "lots" of items. By "lot" I mean many items sold as one "lot." Very few people sell one article of clothing at a time on this site, unless it is a very expensive item (like a Coach purse) or a very large item (like a nice winter coat). So if you're just looking for some new-to-you summer clothes for your family and aren't too particular, Craigslist.com is a great resource! Read the end of Chapter Five first, though, where I give you some guidelines to protect yourself and your money.

- Catalogs are great, as you get to look through them while you leisurely sit on the couch (or somewhere else) and you can put it down to come back to later. Also, you get to see the items on a real person (or maybe not-so-real). I like to browse them to get gift ideas, then see if I can find them cheaper somewhere else (sometimes yes, sometimes no). In general, though, I'm not a catalog person as I'm just too addicted to the internet but I do realize their good qualities! The only thing I recommend is that you first look on the internet to see if 1) you can shop at the store via a rebate website and 2) there are any coupon codes which will knock your total down a bit. Chapter Five tells you how to find such codes.

Eating Out

I could easily say, "Don't eat out as much" but then that would take away from the title of this book ("And Still Have A Life"). You could probably do that easily, say once a month. Make it a date night where you look up recipes, go to the store together to get the ingredients, then cook in the privacy of your kitchen. Depending on what you make, you'll still save money and might even have a decent amount of leftovers. But on with eating out for less.

- If you do nothing else, visit Restaurant.com. You punch in your zip code and see all the restaurants in your area that are offering gift certificates at a discount. The usual amount is $10 for a $25 gift certificate. Now, if you go through a rebate site (visit Chapter Five where I coach you on internet shopping) you'll get a 25% rebate (approximately, depending on the rebate site). Don't stop there, though! Almost always, there are one or more coupon codes for Restaurant.com, with some upwards of 80% off. And there's no shipping fee, of course, because you print them from your own printer. Let's calculate: If you buy one $25 gift certificate for $10, then get 80% off, that puts the checkout total at $2. Then, if you include the 25% rebate (often 27% during the holidays), the final total is $1.50. Many of the gift certificates require a minimum purchase and do not apply to alcohol, tax, or gratuity. But to get a $25 gift certificate for $1.50 is amazing, in my book. If you have friends or family that don't know about the site, you could give them as gifts and have a budget-friendly holiday! Most of the restaurants are locally-owned but I have bought them for Johnny Carino's and Ted's Montana Grill, so I'm sure there are many other corporate-owned restaurants available.

- Certain restaurants have certain specials at certain times. For example, Firebirds Rocky Mountain Grill has a thing called "Wine Down Mondays" where you get half off bottles and glasses of wine all day every Monday. Many places also have "Happy Hour" for drinks and/or appetizers. The individual websites may tell you about them, or you may just have to ask the next time you're in.

- An odd place to check for coupons is the phone book. There is often a green section entitled "coupons" and you just cut them out!

- Visit ValPak.com or check the blue ValPak envelope in your mailbox. There aren't just restaurant coupons, but also coupons for salons, auto care, dental offices, etc. The website lets you print the coupons you need.

- Try ShopAtHome.com. I'll be honest, I haven't actually ever used this site but it looks like something worth checking out.

Electronics

I am all about the internet but sometimes there are certain items where peace of mind is worth not saving an extra twenty or hundred dollars. This is definitely for you to decide but let me provide you with some precautions for buying electronics online or from second-hand sources.

✓ If you buy from the internet, make sure to use PayPal or a credit card which offers some sort of guarantee if the product is defective and you need your money back.

✓ By far one of the best sites I have ever dealt with is Amazon.com. Although they have no store front, their customer service is outstanding, in my opinion. I have only had to return three things. Two of them were picked up by UPS at no charge to me, and the other I couldn't return (long story) but they still gave me my money back! And they have great prices.

✓ Sometimes it's better to go with a larger company name and/or one that has a storefront (i.e. Best-Buy.com, RadioShack.com, etc.). That way, if you need to return the item, you can usually return it to the nearest store.

✓ If you find a great bargain from a site you've never

heard of, search on the internet for the website's name and "reviews." I have actually opted not to purchase from certain sites based on bad reviews and I didn't want to take my chances. But keep in mind, as you read the reviews, that most often the people who review are the few people who had a bad experience. The buyers who had no troubles at all don't say a word.

✓ Except for small, one-function items like flashlights, I strongly recommend going to a physical store to pick out the exact models you like. Play around with them at the store. I'm talking about TVs, MP3 players, alarm clock radios, everything. I purchased an MP3 player online without handling it first and boy, was I disappointed! It turned out to be the most un-user-friendly gadget I have ever dealt with, and I'm pretty technical savvy. The worst part: it was sup-posed to be a gift. I didn't return it, because there wasn't anything "wrong" with it so I wouldn't have gotten a refund. Buyer beware!

✓ If you happen to live in the boonies or don't get out much, and you find a deal on something online, search for reviews on the product itself. Just type in what the item is (including the model number if you have it) and the word "reviews." This system has worked wonders for me since the MP3 player incident.

✓ Make sure to read the fine print to determine the condition of the product. Many sites sell refurbished items. I'm not saying there's anything wrong with buying such items, but if you're looking specifically for a "new" item, you will want to make sure you are not buying used, so look at the fine print.

Okay, so once you have decided your route to discount electronics, here're some websites to try: Amazon.com, BestBuy.com, Buy.com, CircuitCity.com, Crutch-field.com, eBay.com, Frys.com, JR.com, Overstock.com, RadioShack.com, Target.com, TigerDirect.com, Wal-mart.com, and many others of course.

Furniture

A decade ago, I bought furniture to fit my budget and lifestyle- that of a working college girl who moved around a lot. The internet wasn't something I dabbled in much (at all?) so I basically relied on footwork. You can only do so much footwork, though, before you're just ready to go home, so usually I only went to three stores and sometimes only one. The items weren't ones that I meant to last; I just wanted them to work and be cheap.

About six years ago, my now-husband and I started to buy furniture to replace the items that no longer worked or were left behind. We wanted these items to be of better quality, but still within a budget. They were modest pieces: small entertainment center, queen size mattress, couch and loveseat, coffee table set. I had just started to get into the internet a year prior but was still doing a lot of footwork, but more of it. For the entertainment center, we looked at about five stores. The queen mattress took a little longer but I think we finally bought from a sign we saw (not sure they were legal but the mattress was a new pillowtop!) And the couch/coffee table set I found on eBay- one of my first transactions! And a scary one, as it was a "large" purchase, to us. These items fit us and our lifestyle- great quality but still not too bulky.

Four years ago, my husband and I bought our first

house and it was then that we started thinking in terms of longevity. No more particle board or plastic! I had then become proficient at online searching and was introduced to Craigslist.com by our new neighbor. We ended up buying our dining room table from a seller on that site, but not before we looked and looked, and looked again. I wouldn't settle- we knew what we wanted and we could wait till we got it. There is one road about half an hour away that has at least twenty furniture stores in a five mile stretch, no kidding. We took one day and visited every single one of those stores. Then we took another day and drove to High Point, NC which has a gazillion furniture stores. I looked at all my internet sources, then I looked again. We almost went with a set in High Point until the next day I saw a new posting on Craigslist for an older, almost identical set. I bought it the same day, for less than half than I would have paid at the store!

Since the dining room purchase, we have utilized the internet to buy a king-sized bed, large entertainment center, baby furniture, new living room set, etc. etc. If you include the items from Craigslist as "internet purchases," I would venture to say 80% of our furniture pieces were bought online. But that isn't to say we don't do any footwork, oh contraire! We do more footwork now for one piece of furniture than we ever have before.

Speaking of our king-sized bed, I want to share that experience with you. Feel free to skip down to the bullets if you want to keep on... So my husband (who's not petite in any sense) and I started out with a full bed and about three pillows. Then we got a cat and another pillow. Then we purchased a queen bed. Then, a couple years later, we were blessed with another cat and somehow ended up with five pillows on the bed with both cats glued to me at night. Sound familiar? Basically, although by default of his size Rob took up over 1/3 of the bed, he was afraid to move. So we made the decision to get a king bed. We knew this was going to be a purchase for longevity, so we wanted to buy one of those foam mattresses where you can't feel the other person move. Well, I researched and made notes on prices. The most important fact I discovered was that if you didn't use a platform bed or put some sort of solid, flat surface beneath this type of mattress, your warranty might be voided. So then we knew we were looking for a foam mattress and a platform-like bed, and we knew we weren't prepared to fork over more than a thousand dollars. Okay, now I know what you're saying about that budget! "What the heck? You can't even buy a foam mattress for that much! How unrealistic!" But that's the beauty of internet purchases. Set your budget first, then look and look until either a) you find the item within your budget or b) you have exhausted all resources and raise your budget, if possible. Okay, continuing: I realized buying from a regular storefront was out of the question (due to price). I also realized buying from the online outlet centers for those stores was out. Internet furniture dealers were also crossed off due to cost. That left me with two avenues: eBay and Craigslist. I didn't want to buy a used mattress (for personal reasons) and at the time, there were no new mattress sales within our budget on Craigslist. There were some king-sized beds, I remember, but none of them were platform or slatted. (I say slatted because we figured if we bought a bed with slats, we would just put plywood over them.) So what did that leave me with? eBay. Now I saved eBay for last because I knew from previous experience that there are so many furniture items listed it takes awhile to sort through them all. In the end, I found a foam mattress for $400 including shipping. Brand new, king-sized, and about 17" deep. The fine print? It was not of a brand name and it was made of three layers. Sounds funny, I know. I looked at the feedback for the seller to see what other purchasers of the same item had to say: most were great, and the ones that weren't were people who stated they didn't know the mattress was in three pieces. (eBay hint: read every single line of the item description!) We thought and thought, then decided to go for it. $400 blew every other mattress seller out of the water and worst-case-scenario was we turn around a sell it for $150-$200, lesson learned.

Next item to purchase was the bed frame, which I had already narrowed down to eBay for the same reasons as the mattress. This was a little trickier because when it comes to finding furniture on eBay, you have to see what's available, then decide what you want. We had three criteria: 1) platform or slatted 2) modern-looking 3) not too dark. Long story not-as-long, we found two brand new king-sized bed frames, about the same color, from the same seller, for about $400 including shipping. One had a footboard and the other didn't. For various reasons, we went without a footboard. The scary part about such a purchase is you don't know how the quality is going to be. But again, for $400, we took our chances.

Well, we got both items and were thrilled! The bed frame was sturdy- maybe not made of 4x4s like my mother's bed but sturdy nonetheless. And the mattress turned out to be a blessing: I'm not sure how we would have maneuvered a king-sized mattress around our stairs, but our new layered bed came as rolls! We had the option to switch the firm layer with the medium layer depending on our firmness requirements. And lastly, it turns out that I need a super firm mattress because my back started to kill me after sleeping on it. No biggie, though! We stuck some plywood under the first layer on my side and it's perfect, no backache. No wood for Rob, though, and he loves our bed. Had we bought a one-piece foam mattress, we wouldn't have been able to make that easy fix. As a side note, I made those purchases through my rebate site and with a credit card for which I earned points (always do those two things if you can!). So for $800 we had ourselves a customized, brand new king-sized bed. We now have seven pillows, two of which are body-style and we will never go to a smaller bed again.

Here's the gist of that very long story: if you have a small budget to work with, the internet is your best friend. If you aren't willing to take chances, then no chances will ever pay off. And the smaller your budget, the more patience you have to muster. One day, when I'm super rich (ha!) then I will have a larger budget for a bed. Will I make my purchase differently then? Yes. The more you are going to spend, the more I recommend buying from a well-known company which offers warranties; there's more at stake.

What is my point after all that? I've been around the block when it comes to furniture shopping!

- Patience is something you must obtain if you want to save money in this department. So many people walk into a store, fall in love with a couch, and feel they *must* have it the next day! We felt that a living room set is something you have to try out before buying first so we went to five different stores to try them all out. We picked our favorites, got the lowest negotiated prices in writing, then went home to search. We found our most favorite couch for much less from a site called FurnitureDealDirect.com, which I highly recommend! Before buying, though, we took the printout to the store to see if they would hold to their "Price Match Guarantee." Nope! Those guarantees only apply, in general, to other local stores with the same product. The salesman bluntly said, "We can't compete with the internet sites!" So we bought from FurnitureDealDirect.com but had to wait about four weeks for the items. Was it worth it? Absolutely. We definitely got more for our money!

- Don't just go to one store. You may see a table you love at one store, but I'll bet you find a better one at a different store. Use your camera phone to take a picture of the item and the price, then go home and mull it over for at least two days.

- Don't forget discount furniture stores, if you have some nearby. These often sell closeout or display items and you'll be buying the actual item you see, not a new version in a box in the back. I love these stores because the selection is widely varied and the inventory ever changing. So if you exhausted all these stores your first go round, try them again a month later, or ask the salesperson when the next shipment is.

- Large devoted stores like Rooms To Go, The Room Store, Ashley Furniture, Haverty's, etc. have great sales when they need to make room for the next wave of furniture. I think the only way to find out when that is is to call or ask a salesperson (find out when the shipment comes in, then shop the week before). So, if you're loyal to a certain storefront, this may be your route.

- This may be a myth but someone named Sam gave me this advice for all commissioned products (cars, etc.). He said to shop at the end of the month as the salespeople need to make their quota and are anxious to deal with you. Translation: the price may be more negotiable at the end of the month.

- Something I have personally experienced is a salesperson changing their tune as I'm leaving. It's kind of like the advice I gave on credit cards; you act like you're going to cancel/ walk out without buying and they start pulling aces out of their sleeves. So even if you *know* you're going to buy an item, *pretend* that it's too expensive and you need to think about it. No guarantees from me, but it's worth a shot.

- For items that you don't need to try out first, such as end tables and headboards, I definitely recommend the internet. Without spending gas money, you can browse literally thousands of items. Shipping cost is a factor, but the prices online are usually so much lower that it's still a savings. These types of pieces often come "Assembly Required" so keep that in mind if you don't consider yourself handy. I do suggest having a clear idea of what you're wanting. If you just type the words "end table' into your search engine, you will be overwhelmed and will close the window. So search, instead, for (without quotation marks) "end table light wood drawer" or "desk metal dark wood" or "headboard cherry wood sleigh". You'll still end up with a lot of results, as there are numerous online furniture stores, but they will be much more manageable. For more coaching on internet searching, read Chapter Five.

- Don't forget Craigslist. For our coffee table, we wanted something to match our décor with drawers and made of solid wood. But we didn't want to spend an arm and a leg and we didn't mind if it had a few scratches as it was bound to get more from our toddler. We found the perfect item, but only after I had looked every day for five days. There are so many people listing on Craigslist that if you don't see the item you want one day, you *need* to look again the next day. And if you see a really high quality item you need to act fast as good pieces go quick!

- For "Assembly Required" pieces of furniture, eBay is a great resource. You may think that the auction site is so inundated with items that you don't know how to begin searching, but the folks there have actually made it very simple to sift through the billions of products. Read Chapter Six where I go into more depth with eBay guidance.

- Thrift shops are also good places to check out, especially if you know they pick up donated items. A good example is the Durham Rescue Mission which picked up our large, solid wood entertainment center (sadly, we had no room for it in our new place) for free and gave us a donation receipt. I know items like that end up in their thrift shop from which the proceeds go back to the mission. So internet search for "furniture donation pick-up" (no quotations) and your city's name, or go straight to the site for your local Habitat for Humanity, Goodwill (GCF), or rescue mission. Often, the sites will not only give information about donating, they'll also point you to their thrift stores. Again, the inventory at these shops change so check back if you don't score the first time.

- Garage sales are a hidden treasure. And I mean "hidden" like you have to hunt them out and actually go to them. But the people holding these sales are wanting to get rid of the stuff they have and usually, when it comes to large pieces of furniture, they don't have the ability to move it (no truck) so they're anxious to have someone take it off their hands for them. While I know there are different types of sellers out there, I think the majority price their items higher than what they'll actually take because they know buyers are going to haggle. So definitely negotiate price; worst case scenario is the seller is firm. But you must have the time and the patience to go from sale to sale, and even weekend to weekend. Of all the tips I have listed, if you can do this one, you will save the most money!

- Websites to try: Craigslist.com, DirectlyHome.com, eBay.com, Furniture.com, FurnitureDeal-Direct.com, FurnitureESuperstore.com, Furniture-OnTheWeb.com, Overstock.com, RoomsToGo.com, RoomStore.com, TheFurnitureWarehouse.net, etc.

Gift Cards

If I had to pick one section for you to read and forget all the others, it would be this one. So listen up.

The next time you go to a store and buy a gift card,

just know that you are wasting money! There are multitudes of websites devoted to selling gift cards- they work kind of like car dealerships. The website buys them from someone who just wants the cash and pays them roughly 75% of the card's value. Then the site resells that gift card to people like me for about 85% of the card's value. eBay works a little differently; those people just wanting cash skip the middleman and recoup a little more of the value.

You shouldn't just buy gift cards to give as gifts! There are cards for restaurants that you can use yourself, cards for grocery stores, cards for department stores, etc.

Seriously, you need to consider these websites:
ABCGiftCards.com
CityDeals.com
eBay.com
GiftCard
Rescue.com
GiftCards4Less.com
GiftCardsAgain.com
GiftCardSwapping.com
MonsterGiftCard.com
PlasticJungle.com
StarGiftCardExchange.com
SwapAGift.com, etc.

Greeting Cards

Have you perused the card aisle lately and thought, "These are all the same!" or "None of these fit!"? I gave up on greeting cards a long time ago so I either don't give any or I make my own. That way, I don't feel so bad if the recipient throws my card away (since I didn't spend four dollars on it). Or, to be more optimistic, I can say exactly the right thing.

If you aren't the creative type, there are several templates available on Microsoft.com and perhaps more included with your Publisher program. Or, spend time just designing one and save it as your own template. You can either buy special greeting card paper or use plain paper, depending on your recipient!

This may sound like a cheesy way to save money but I actually think my family now looks forward to my cards (when I give them).

Landscaping & Gardening

This topic is dear to my heart, as I love gardening. I wouldn't necessarily say I'm good at it, but I'm new and learning. In my apartment in Wisconsin, I had a large balcony on which my now-husband built a four by five garden. I grew dwarf varieties of tomatoes, green beans, carrots, jalapenos, and something else I can't remember. It was the best garden I have ever grown! I think it had to do with being on the second floor in Wisconsin which equates to very few pests. My last place was a townhouse with a workable eight by six plot in the back. It was also an end unit (so it had some room on the side to play with) and in front there was a great area for flowers. So believe me when I say I know how expensive landscaping and gardening are, and I didn't even have a lawn to mow! I can't imagine how much money I would have spent if I had had a house like my mother's with a huge yard.

If you're a seasoned gardener, don't like gardening, or don't have anywhere to garden, then you can skip this section if you'd like! But here're a few tricks I picked up along my on-going journey:

- If you'd like to save money in the long run, buy perennials. I put bulbs in the front of my townhouse because I didn't want to mess with planting the front every year when I was so busy with the back. Here's a bulb worth spending money on: canna lily. They are hardy as all get out, albeit very tall. Asiatic Lilies are awesome, too.

- If you just want maintenance-free flowers, find self-sowing flowers for your zone. Usually these are the wildflower sort... When I moved into my townhouse, I tore out all the dead Black-Eyed Susans. I was still finding new sprouts three years later!

- If it's a maintenance-free garden you want (ha!), try just planting herbs and tomatoes. Many herbs act as perennials in southern zones and tomatoes are very easy to grow and naturally pest resistant. For a sure-fire herb you will rue planting, try mint- any smell. I had a chocolate mint plant that I could not get rid of. It's not that I didn't like it - it makes a great tea and smells wonderful. It's just that I wanted the space and it was somewhat invasive. I suppose that's why the pros advise to keep mint in containers!

- Regarding a garden, be familiar with the common pests in your area and have your plan of action and weapons ready *before* you plant. If you don't, your money will be wasted! It would be worth your time to research companion planting (i.e. carrots and tomatoes but not dill and tomatoes) as well as the best way to get rid of pests. The two biggest foes in my garden were aphids and squash vine borers. If you aren't ready for them, you will sadly watch your expensive garden perish.

- Know what grows when and where. I don't know why the stores even sell bell peppers here in NC. I suppose some people (more experienced than I) can get winners but I had nothing but blossom drop due to the high temperatures at night. Some plants can handle frost (like winter squashes) and others can't handle the extreme heat (like snap peas). If you have money to throw away, then plant willy nilly. If not, conduct a little free internet research before buying and planting.

- If you have an area in which everything dies (no sun, too much sun, no drainage, pure clay, etc.) then quit trying to put the wrong plants there! You will waste a lot of money on plants that are just going to die. Your time would be well spent researching plants which will grow in such conditions. I bought and followed the advice of a book on plants for the state where I live and those plants have thrived! Chances are, there's a book for your state, as well.

- To make your money go even farther, buy plants that are easy to propagate so that you only have to buy one or two as "parents". One example is Forsythia; you can bend a stalk downward, bury the end or middle in the soil, and soon you will have new root formation! Then you can transplant the "daughter." Strawberries send out runners, and Asiatic Lilies grow bigger and bigger bulbs which you can separate every year.

- Follow the planting directions! When I first started

planting, I put the plants where I thought they'd look best, not where they would thrive. So I ended up with hostas on one side of the yard but not the other. In fact, on the "other" sunny side was a bare spot where the hostas were supposed to grow back from. I should have spent my money, instead, on plants that enjoy "full sun." Also, as an example, if the directions say to soak the bulbs or seeds first before planting, you should probably do so. I'm not saying all the rules are set in stone but if you're a newbie like me, your money will go farther by following the directions until your black thumb turns into a green thumb.

- If you haven't discovered Monkey Grass (aka Mondo Grass) and Liriope, you don't know what you're missing! Apart from trying to grow it inside, I am positive this plant will withstand anything. Before I knew better, I was trimming the plants and threw the undesirables onto a low-growing groundcover juniper bush. My thoughts: they would die and provide natural fertilizer. Not so! They actually, somehow, survived and took root amidst the juniper (not a good combination, FYI). Ours acted as a border; they were subjected to the full North Carolina sun with no watering by us and they thrived, producing their tiny purple flowers. Sometimes we would give them "flat tops" with a weed whacker and they looked great. Plus, they divide superbly.

- This doesn't quite fit the topic but there really isn't anywhere else to discuss indoor plants. I really only have one piece of advice: buy plants that are labeled "low light." In Cristy language, this translates to "low maintenance." I am very neglectful of houseplants but I have managed to keep the same eight potted plants alive for several years! All of them are "low light" and can go weeks without watering (not that I recommend doing that on purpose). And I have even managed to create new plants from some of them! Take a snip and place the cutting in water until you see a sizeable amount of roots, then plant the little guy. Few, if any, are flowering plants but they make great foliage.

Want websites for mail-order plants? Blooming-Bulb.com, Brecks.com, Garderners.com, GardensAlive.com, Gurneys.com, HenryFields.com, SpringHillNursery.com, TastefulGarden.com, etc.

Magazines & Newspapers

This is going to be a sore spot for some people, as I am fully aware of the predicament many newspapers are now in. With a large percentage of people going to the internet for "free" news, it's currently a small percentage that turns to the tangible copy. On one hand, I feel for the newspaper companies, but on the other hand I think it's business as usual. Mobile phone manufacturers have to keep up with the latest touch-screen technology in order to survive. Car manufacturers must now think about hybrids and electrics to keep their heads above the water. So, too, should the newspaper printers find their new, profitable niche in this digital world. With that said, I continue:

- Do you *really* read your newspaper? I mean, do you read enough of it to justify the amount you spend on it? I can think of three people I know, right off the bat, who do in fact read the paper from cover to cover each day. Admirable! But for each of those three, I can think of five (at least) who end up throwing their unread stacks in the recycle bin (hopefully, and not the trash).

- If you use the daily news for its daily crossword puzzle, consider cancelling or reducing your subscription and printing the crosswords free from the internet.

- If you read a smidgen here or there or only read certain sections, consider cancelling or reducing your subscription and setting your internet homepage to that newspaper's website. Every time you open your browser, you'll be reminded that you're supposed to do some reading.

- If you are like my father and do, actually, read the printed paper then good for you for supporting it! I am not certain how you can get a better rate besides maybe calling the company. But from what I've seen the cost is not that great so maybe your saving efforts should go elsewhere since this is a service you thoroughly use. If you're determined, though, try DiscountedNewspapers.com or type "discount newspapers" into your search engine.

- Now, for magazines: if you buy a certain magazine from a check-out stand three or more times a year, then you should just get a subscription (but only if you shop through certain sites, keep reading). You will definitely spend more by buying one at a time.

- If you subscribe to magazines, you should shop through a large magazine site such as BestDeal-Magazines.com, BlueDolphin.com, DiscountMagazines.com, DiscountMags.com, eMagazines.com, Magazines.com, MagMall.com, ValueMags.com, etc. etc. I just picked a few from a slew of results by typing "discount magazine" into my search bar. Make sure you go through a rebates site, though, as these magazine companies often offer large rebates, up to 30%! (Read Chapter Five)

- When you subscribe to a magazine, I suggest saying it's a gift. There's usually an option for this when you check out and the fine print says this means the subscription won't automatically be renewed. I found this out the hard way; I had subscribed and got a great deal but then... after a year the subscription was automatically renewed at the regular price! I then cancelled and only got a prorated refund. Supposedly they sent me an email stating the renewal was about to take place, but that must have been filtered out by my junk box. It's cheaper to let the subscription run out, as the magazine then gets desperate for you to buy again and offers you a fantastic deal. Or you can find it even cheaper somewhere else. Never pay full price!!

- Get real about the subscriptions you currently have. My husband gets a reputable magazine sent weekly. He had great intentions when he ordered it but quickly fell behind due to school and our son. Those magazines (wonderful reading material) are just piling up. You can bet I'm not renewing! I also know of two people who have multiple monthly magazine subscriptions, and I know those two people do not read them all. Figure out which ones you read and which ones you don't. For the ones you don't, call the company and see if you can get a prorated refund and definitely don't renew.

- Having nothing to do with saving money, I implore you to recycle your newspapers and magazines rather than throwing them away. Just like the car companies, we should change our behaviors to be more respectful of the earth, as well.

Movie Rentals

This is where it's at, in my opinion. With increasing competition, the package prices for online movie rentals are great!

- Blockbuster offers many ways to get free rentals. For a summary of these offers, visit this site from ScoreADeal.com:

  http://www.scoreadeal.com/coupons/blockbuster.asp.
- Online rentals are awesome, and a great bargain! I love that I can browse previews at home, put the movies in order of preference, and not have to visit a brick-and-mortar store. When I see a new movie in the mail, I actually get excited! To date, Blockbuster.com and Netflix.com are the only mail-order movie rental sites I'm aware of.
- A hot new sensation is movie rental kiosks, usually found at grocery stores. The only two companies that I am aware of are RedBox.com and MovieCube.com-there may be more! For one dollar a night, you can rent a new release from one of these convenient kiosks, which is quite a bargain. Look for them at your nearest grocery store and try it out; they're very user-friendly and almost too simple. When I returned a

DVD for the first time, I stood there waiting for it to give me further instructions or spit out a receipt but there were none. If you sign up online, both the websites give you one free rental using a promotional code sent via email. Just be ready to have a line quickly form behind you if you go on a weekend evening!

- If you don't have a RedBox or MovieCube (or similar) kiosk nearby, and don't watch enough movies (or watch them consistently enough) to justify an online subscription, then maybe it would be more cost-effective for you to use the Pay-Per-View option on your cable. I really can't go into more detail, as I don't know much about them, but I do know you can get them for as little as $2.99 a pop.

- If you're hankering to watch something other than TV but don't feel like going out, check out a TV series you haven't heard of or catch up on your favorite dramas. Visit ABC.com, NBC.com, CBS.com, Fox.com, CWTV.com, or the website of your favorite channel. For most, if not all, you can watch past episodes for free on your computer. You could pick a new series and watch for hours on end!

Movie Theaters

Does anyone else remember the reasonable movie ticket prices back in the day? Frankly, I have decided it's just not worth the money anymore! But, I realize I'm in the minority and you still want your movie-going life so here're some things to think about:

- If you have a cheap/budget/dollar movie theater near you, why would you even think about going to the fancy, new, expensive one? Well, apart from the new movies and stadium seating... Just think: if you always opted for the budget theater, you could go more often and still spend less money!

- As everyone knows, matinee movies are cheaper. I think every theater has different matinee hours but you'd play it safe by going on a weekday afternoon.
- Do an internet search for "free movie tickets" or "discounted movie tickets" (no quotations) and you'll get a bunch of sites supposedly telling you how to get such items. From what I could tell, most talk about signing-up for and attending screenings so...
- Do an internet search for "movie screenings" and you may just hit the jackpot!
- I would say bring your own candy but that's against the rules................
- If you eat before the movie, you'll be less inclined to pay the exorbitant prices on candy and popcorn.

Vacations

So if you're like me, the reason you save money is so you can take a vacation or two each year. But no one says you can't save on the vacation itself!

To preface, when I say "travel site," I am referring to the following (in alphabetical order): BestFares.com, Expedia.com, Hotwire.com, Kayak.com, LowFares.com, Orbitz.com, Priceline.com, SideStep.com, Travelocity.com, TravelZoo.com, TripAdvisor.com, and there may be a couple other not-so-known sites. When I say "airline site," then I mean the website of the airline of your choice. If I say "hotel booking site," I am indicating Booking.com, Hotel.info, HotelReservation.com, Hotels.com, Quick-

Book.com, Otel.com, RoomSaver.com, etc. And finally, for "car rental site" I suggest CarRentalExpress.com, CarRentals.com, E-ZRentACar.com, RentACar.com, RentalCarMomma.com, RentalCars.com, USave.com, VroomVroomVroom.com, etc.

- In the last couple years, I have never taken a vacation that didn't take at least three hours to research and purchase. I am way too committed to getting the best quality for the best price to be anything other than diligent. I will search every single site with multiple browser windows open. If you are serious about saving money, you will reserve a nice chunk of time to do so!
- You may think that the travel sites are only for airfares but not so! On many of these sites, you can also search for hotels only, cars only, and any combination.
- These instructions are similar to searching for an item to purchase so visit Chapter Five if you think visuals will help you follow along:
  1. Open three or four browser windows on your computer. On each one, go to a different travel site.
  2. Starting with the first window, punch in your travel requirements (dates, times, etc.) and get to the checkout site where you know the final total.
  3. Do this with the other windows, as well.
  4. Close all the windows EXCEPT the cheapest one.
  5. Keep opening and closing travel sites until you have found the definite winner.

6. Now open a new window, and go to the rebate site you now use to make all your online purchases with. Hopefully, the travel site with the lowest price will be listed. Open the travel site through the rebate site, then close the other one (the travel site *not* through the rebate site). You may have to punch in your info again, or you may not.

7. Check the rebate site to see if they list a coupon code, then check the internet to see if there's a better one (read Chapter Five for more information on coupon codes).

- If there were two or more sites which had similar rates, you might keep them all open until you have played around with the coupon codes. There are variations of this "method" (like opening all the sites at once or going through the rebate site first, and not last) so you just do what works for you!

- If you are buying a package of some sort (flight + car, flight + hotel + car, etc.) then I'd put money on the travel site being the best deal, rather than purchasing all the services separately. But you could definitely check them out separately!

- If you are buying an airline ticket only, you may have noticed a trend where the same airline was consistently the lowest fare. Go to the website of this airline and see if the fare is cheaper off the main site itself. Twice I have found this to be the case!

- If you are reserving a hotel only, then you will want to compare hotel booking sites. Follow the same instructions above to determine the lowest priced site; you can either do this before or after the travel sites, but I recommend checking them all.

- Same goes for the car rentals: check out both car rental sites and travel sites.
- I don't really know where to put this so I'll stick it here. I suggest paying for your rental car with a Visa credit card. That way, when you go to the counter to pay for and pick up the car, you can confidently decline the insurance they offer you. Most Visa cards (read your agreement or call their 800 number to confirm whether yours qualifies) automatically provide you with rental car insurance, provided you pay for the rental with that card. Often, these same cards provide insurance for air travel as well.
- If you only need airline tickets, type "cheap flights" (no quotations) into your search engine and you'll come up with a lot (too many to list) of websites to help you find discounted tickets.
- Ebay and Craigslist are also savings avenues you probably haven't thought about. Chances are, if you have a specific destination, you won't get very far with this route. But if you're open to go just about anywhere, see what you can find! A lot of people can't get credit for flights they won't/can't use or want the money for a voucher they received.
- A new rage which has emerged in the last several years is home swapping (not to be confused with house trading, which is more a real estate thing). you can either stay in someone's house while they stay in yours, stay in someone's house while they vacation elsewhere, or you can just find a really cool rental property. Considering how much I spend on vacations (not a lot!), I don't consider these to be a real bargain, UNLESS you literally swap. If you don't

swap, just remain open-minded and be diligent with your search, and you may find a diamond in the rough or the place you are willing to spend your hard-saved money on! Sites: 1stHomeExchange.com, 4HomeEx.com, ExchangeHomesOIA.com, Home-Exchange.com, HomeExchangeVacation.com, HomeForSwap.com, HomeLink-USA.com, etc. etc. Type "home exchange" or something similar into your search engine!

- Alright, last bullet. My shout out goes to Hotwire.com for the amazing car rental deal I received! Thanks!!

Chapter Five

How to Shop on the Internet

There really is an art to this. I won't claim to be a professional, but only because I haven't competed with others who claim to be good. I do know of a lot of avenues, though, that the average person does not take advantage of. Here goes:

Use a Rebate Site

I don't care which one you use, just use one! If you don't you are missing out on free money. I say this because you're not buying items *on* the rebate site, you're buying items *through* the site and they're items you were going to buy anyway. For instance, I buy my cats' food supplements and treats on the internet because it's cheaper. I could either go through the rebate site and get 3% cashback, or I could not. What is the smarter choice there? Any and every time you are going to purchase something on the internet, go through the rebate site if you can. The only exception that I am aware of (besides smaller, more obscure sites) is Amazon.com. This website does not offer cash-back rebates, at least not for my rebate site (and not at this point, hint hint Amazon), but there are many sales and coupon codes listed.

These rebate sites are in alphabetical order: Big-Crumbs.com, eBates.com, ExtraBux.com, FatWallet.com, GreenBackStreet.com, MoreRebates.com, MrRebates.com, RebateShare.com, Spree.com, and there may be others. For once, I will say which one I use: MrRebates.com. I have been shopping through this site since the beginning of 2007 and to date have received over $350 in checks, with over $100 waiting to post. So if you want to skip the shopping around and go with a site that comes highly recommended (by me), then just use MrRebates.com. It is also a member of the Better Business Bureau with an A grading. I'm certain the other sites are just as notable, but since I haven't used them myself I can't speak for them! So, when I am giving pointers for shopping on a rebate site, I am specifically using my experience with MrRebates.com as the model and other sites will vary widely, most likely.

- Many rebate sites offer a registration bonus, meaning you'll automatically have x amount added to your account once you sign up. For Mr. Rebates, it's $5. They're paying you to participate!!
- You can view all stores, search for a particular store, or see all stores within a certain category. I never use the view "all stores" button as that is just too overwhelming. However, I have searched for a particular store when I know of the exact store I want to buy from (i.e. eBay.com). When it's not the store that's important, but rather a group of similar items (i.e. car rental sites), then I'll click on the "travel" category and arrange the stores by cash-back percentage, highest to lowest.

- If you don't care so much what the store is, but only that you get a certain item for the cheapest price, then you can do a product search as opposed to a store search. When you type the product into the search bar, you will see which stores (affiliated with the rebate site) carry that item and for how much. Be skeptical, though; on many occasions I have discovered other stores which carry the item which weren't displayed as results.

- You have to click through the rebate site and finish your purchase in the same window. If you close it, start anew, and/or delete your cookies during your shopping session, you will not be credited for the rebate.

- If you are clicking through to an auction site like eBay.com, your WINNING bid must have been made on the click through in order to get credit. In other words, it's not the payment of the item that counts, it's the bid.

- Rebates take approximately three months from the posting date to become available. You can usually see them within a few days of purchasing, but they will say "Pending" (and may take even longer to post). Once the three month period ends, they then become "Available." The reason for this delay is to account for any transaction changes, such as partial credits and refunds.

- When you have a minimum of ten dollars as "Available," then you may request a payment, which will be processed at the beginning of the next month. You can request a PayPal payment or payment via real check in the mail.

- Please remember, I make no guarantees as to these figures; I have seen percentages change, stores added and removed, and the site retains all rights to change those figures at any time. Also, each rebate site has its own numbers, obviously.

To reiterate, IF YOU ARE NOT USING A RE-BATE SITE YOU ARE MISSING OUT ON FREE MONEY!

A shot of Mr. Rebates' homepage

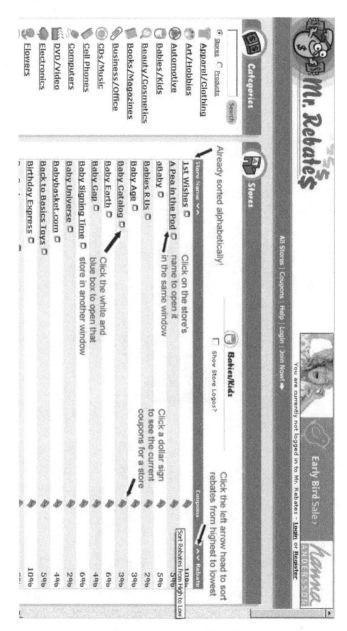

The site is very user-friendly!

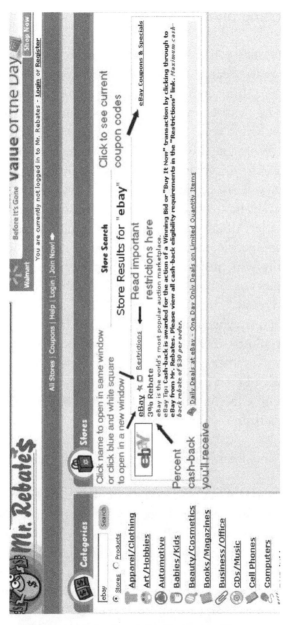

How to read the detailed information for a store

Searching on the Internet

I'm sure you've done a search on one or more of the popular search engines: AltaVista.com, AOL.com, Ask.com, Bing.com, DogPile.com, Google.com, Lycos.com, MetaCrawler.com, MSN.com, WebCrawler.com, Yahoo.com. As I usually say, I'm sure I've missed many. What I'm also sure of is that when you conducted that search, you came up with some 90,000+ results. Of course, you trust that your search engine will put the most relevant at the top. But the more specific you can be, the less time you will spend browsing. To help you be more specific, there are "tools" you can use, which are basically punctuation marks. If you find the following examples confusing, there is a chart in Chapter Seven to make it easy.

Let's say you want a desk lamp, with a lampshade. You would rather have it in a cherry colored wood tone, and you'd rather not have any of the major components be made of metal. If your search engine has an "images" selection, click on that and then type this, exactly, including the quotations:

"desk lamp" lampshade "cherry wood" –metal

If you don't put quotations around "desk lamp" you will get sites for both desks and lamps, not just lamps. Then browse through the images to see if any of them strike your fancy. If one does, you should be able to click on the image in order to go to the site. If you don't find one you like, play around with your search (using quotations and the minus sign) until you do. When you find the one you want, try to find a model number and/or brand name and description, and *then* try to find the best deal, which I will go into in a bit.

If you're looking for an item for which looks aren't important, but features are, then use the same advice but type it into your "web" and not the "images." For example, pretend you are interested in a book light. You saw one in the store that hooks up to the computer via USB but can also be powered with 2 AA batteries. You liked the clip feature to hook onto a book. What are all the ways such a light would be described? Book light, computer light, travel light. Here's what I would type:

book computer OR travel light USB "AA batteries" clip

- I did not put an "OR" between book and computer because I want to use it for both, not either. Book lights are usually only battery powered, and computer lights are usually only USB powered.
- I put "travel" in there to see if the results showed any cool foldable ones. You could take this out if that wasn't important.
- "Light" is there because I definitely need this word in the results. You could also type "LED" if that's the kind of bulb you wanted. I wouldn't use quotations around that, though because some sites will say "LED light," others will say "LED book light" and still others will just say "LED" in the description.
- "USB" is a keyword because this is not an option, just like "light."
- "AA batteries" is in quotations for two reasons: 1) I don't want any lights that require some crazy type of battery, like a watch-type battery. 2) I don't want any listings to come up that say something like, "Re-

quires no batteries." If I don't put "AA" in there, such results will come up because, according to the search engine, that word is present, albeit not in the way I want.

- I put "clip" in the search because this was a feature I felt was really important. If I decide it's not, then I can take it off!

If you do the search as book computer OR travel light USB "AA batteries" clip, you will still get around 7,000 results. Take off "clip" and you're back up to 25,000. Add "folds" and you're down to 3,000. Other qualities to consider are flexible neck, number of light bulbs, number of batteries, color, travel case, etc. I suggest writing down all the optimal qualities and putting all of those into your search first, before playing around with the search words. You may just get exactly what you want!

NOW: After you have decided which light (or lamp) is the cream of the crop, *then* you go on to find it for the cheapest price.

Finding the Best Deal

I'm going to go through two examples...

Example #1: Okay, let's continue with the book light example. Let me disclaim that I do not have the light I chose for this example, nor do I have a need for this type of light. I am only using it as an example, and I picked it at random! Lucky them.... Okay, let's say I chose the Verilux Book & Travel Deluxe Natural Spectrum Reading Light with an SKU/ model number of VB01JJ4 on the Verilux website. On this site, it retails for $19.95.

- Open five internet tabs or windows.
  1. Main search engine
  2. Rebate site
  3. eBay.com
  4. Amazon.com
  5. The website of the manufacturer, in this case Verilux.com
- On your main search engine, click on the "Shopping" link. Type"Verilux VB01JJ4" (no quotations). Then arrange the results from lowest to highest price. I see the cheapest one is $18.80. I open that link and find shipping from that site (of which I've never heard) is $7.95.
- On the rebate site, click the option for products. Type "Verilux VB01JJ4" (no quotations). I see there are no results. I do a store search for "Verilux" and discover they are not a rebate vendor. I leave the window open in case the site I ultimately choose to buy from does offer rebates.
- On eBay I type "Verilux VB01JJ4" (without quotations) and discover no results. I think to myself, I bet a lot of sellers wouldn't put the SKU in the item title. So I click the option below the search box which reads, "Include title and description." I then see three results, all of which are $19.95 with $5.95 shipping. So I try "verilux book light" (without quotations) and see a few more results, one of which is the one I want. But they're selling it for $24.95 with free shipping. It is brand new and from a Power Seller. (Read more on eBay buying in Chapter Six.)
- On Amazon I type "Verilux VB01JJ4" and find that it is $19.95 from Verilux. Shipping is free if I spend

$25 or more, otherwise it is $5.31 to ship. (Note: I couldn't determine this shipping charge until I acted like I was checking out. This is common!) If I look further at the description screen, I see some small words reading "10 new from $7.96" and think I should check that out! (That option is in small print, about two inches below the big-printed price). So I click on that link and am first confused. I still only see $19.95! Then I realize they are listing their "featured merchants" at the top. Scroll down. Ah, there it is: a NEW one for $7.96 with $5.99 shipping from a merchant I've never heard of. I add it to my cart and move on.

- At the manufacturer's website, I see it is, of course, $19.95 with $5.95 shipping.

Okay, at this point you have many options. You could keep searching for the cheapest item, using other search engines and exhausting your brain. I personally wouldn't do this because it's apparent there isn't much variation in the price across the board and I think you'd be wasting your time. I decide to go with Amazon and here is how I came to that conclusion:

1. I'm going to close this first tab. First flag: I've never heard of this site. Now, I have, on multiple occasions, taken chances and bought from obscure sites. Only do this if you are going to purchase with a credit card (not debit) or, preferably, PayPal. That way, if your chancing doesn't pay off, you can make a claim. So the real, more important, reason I'm not going to use this one is the total price is $26.75, which is more than all the other sites. Important lesson here! Many

sites offer a lower item price but get you on the shipping! So ALWAYS factor in the shipping cost.

2. I will close the rebate site but only after I decided to go with Amazon. See, Amazon doesn't offer rebates.... tsk tsk, but I suppose they make enough money they don't have to. If I were going through eBay, I would have opened eBay again though this site to get my 3% rebate.

3. I'm closing eBay.com because I opted for Amazon.

4. This tab I'll leave open because I found it for approximately $11 cheaper. Now, I did mention that I've never heard of the seller but... it is listed as new and I feel safe because Amazon is wonderful at taking care of their customers, in my opinion. No matter your payment method, if you bought it from them and have an issue, I'd bet money that they'd rectify the problem.

5. Obviously, I close the Verilux tab.

Let's pretend that I didn't find the bargain on Amazon and I pretty much was going to pay the same amount. Then, which would I choose?

✓ I would still choose Amazon. There is always something I "need" and I would find something worth $5.05 (with free shipping over $25) to make it so I didn't "waste" my money on shipping.

✓ As a second choice, I would choose the Verilux site itself. If you include the 3% rebate I would receive on ebay for the $24.95 item, I would spend about $2 more going this route, which completely goes against the title of this book. My reason: Verilux offers a return policy within thirty days and they will provide you with a pre-paid shipping label. Read more about return policies later in this chapter under Precautions.

✓ If the price was significantly lower, then I would go with eBay, but only if the seller offered a return policy. This is important! For all electronics, you want a good return policy because you'll never know if you got the one item with the bum cord or light until it's actually in your hands. In this case, eBay is last because although the seller offers a return policy within thirty days, the buyer has to pay the shipping for that return. I have been hit with that before and the two bucks extra via the manufacturer is worth paying for peace of mind.

✓ As a last resort, I would check a physical store like the Sharper Image and bypass shipping altogether.

Example #2: Now I want to go into an example using coupon codes and actually getting a great deal! The next section in this chapter will help you find such coupon codes, but I want to motivate you first. Okay, for this I will use cat treats, and my standard quantity for searching will be 15, as I like to buy in bulk when I can. In stores, I've seen them priced between $2.99 and $3.99 per package.

• Open six internet tabs or windows.
  1. Main search engine
  2. Main search engine
  3. Rebate site
  4. eBay.com
  5. Amazon.com

6. The website of the manufacturer, in this case Greenies.com.

- On your first main search engine window, click on the "Shopping" link. Type "Greenies feline" (no quotations). Then arrange the results from lowest to highest price. I see the cheapest price is $1.75 each. I open that link and find shipping from that site (of which I've never heard and self-proclaims to be brand new) is $8.60. Also, the site lists them even cheaper, at $1.65 each. They immediately offer a coupon code for 10% off, which brings the total to $30.87.

- On the second main search engine tab, I check out the next four or five sites with the lowest prices and determine they are more expensive when shipping is included. Again, many sites lower the items prices and stick you with a higher shipping charge. So I close this window.

- On the rebate site, click the option for products. Type "Greenies feline" (no quotations). I see there are 33 items from five stores. I look at the prices and determine Drs. Foster and Smith (DrsFosterSmith.com) have the lowest price, at $2.29 each. I open a new window for that store *through* the rebate site and determine my total cost. I find they offer a three pack for $5.99 and free shipping! Without a coupon code, my total is $29.95.

- On eBay I type "Greenies feline" (without quotations) and discover many results. The cheapest is $2.99 each. One would think I would automatically close this window, but I know from experience that many sellers offer combined shipping, so it may be worth checking out. In this particular case, the combined shipping rate for 15 packs is $16.50. Ridiculous. I close this window.

- On Amazon I type "Greenies feline" and see that the lowest price is $0.19 each with $4.99 shipping. That does not make sense.... Plus, the ounces are wrong; the description says nine ounces when I think only three ounce packages are sold. Unless it's for three packs of three ounces, in which case the $0.19 price tag makes even less sense. Thinking I might take advantage of something super, I put a whole bunch in my cart and go to check out. Turns out, the $4.99 shipping charge is PER PACKAGE! So my shipping fee ends up being over $100. Be careful!
- Okay, starting over on Amazon and ignoring the $0.19 one, I find the lowest price to be $1.88. Total price for 15 packages with shipping is $34.69. More than Drs. Foster and Smith, so I close this window.
- At the manufacturer's website, Greenies.com, they aren't listed for sale. Instead, the site provides a store locator. I punch in my zip code and see many stores listed. Since I have the time and I love to be thorough, I check all of the websites. Still, all are more expensive than Drs. Foster and Smith. I close this window.

At the end of this, I am left with three windows open. One is the site I found from my search engine ($30.87), one is the rebate site, and the last is Drs. Foster and Smith which I opened *through* the rebate site ($29.95 plus a 6% cash-back). Now, I already entered a coupon code with the first site (which is not a rebate vendor), but I'm going to search for a better one, as well as one for Drs. Foster and Smith (read up on "Finding Coupon Codes" which is the next section). My results:

✓ For the first site, I find a coupon code for 15% off (rather than just 10%), bringing my total to $29.64.
✓ For Drs. Foster and Smith, I find a coupon code for $5 off any order, bringing my total to $24.95. Looks like this is the winner! I close the first site and purchase my Greenies, receiving my $1.50 cash-back rebate.

Let's calculate: I ultimately purchased these treats for $1.56 each. If I had purchased these at the store for $2.99 each, I would have spent $44.85 plus tax. If they were $3.99 a pack, I would have spent $59.85 plus tax. So I saved somewhere between $22 and $37, roughly. Notice the power of buying in bulk, rather than impulse buying at the store when you run out.

Finding Coupon Codes

The first place to look when searching for coupon codes is your rebate site.

- If you see one for free shipping then don't waste your time searching for any others except if 1) the website lets you use more than one coupon code and/or 2) the website gives you free shipping already.
- If you see one for 15% off any order, then I wouldn't look any further. The odds of finding a code for anything more than that are very slim, with the exception of Kohls.com and Restaurant.com.
- Don't bother looking for a coupon code for Walmart.com. At this point in time, the site does not ac-

cept online codes. They do, however, offer cash-back through many rebate sites (i.e. 3% via Mr. Rebates) as well as free site-to-store shipping.

- Another site for which generic coupon codes do not exist is Amazon.com. By "generic" I mean a coupon code that is good for any order. There are coupon codes, though, for certain items on the site. So while Amazon.com offers no cash-back rebate through the rebate site, they are often still a listed vendor. So check to see if the item you're purchasing currently has a sale on it!

Never assume your rebate site has listed all the available coupon codes. I will be so bold as to say this is never the case. In my above example of the Greenies I bought from Drs. Foster and Smith, my rebate site had no real coupon codes to speak of. So I went to my search engine and found a whole slew of them.

- The easiest way to find a coupon code, I think, is to type the store name and the words "coupon code" (no quotations) into your search engine. Then I browse through the first five results or so.
- If you're feeling lucky, you could add a percentage to your search. For instance:

   'store name' coupon code 15% off

   Add quotations if you feel the need; I rarely do.

- Another easy way to find them is by going directly to a coupon code site. They must make money by pay-per-clicks but that knowledge doesn't interest me. What's great about most of these sites is they bluntly list the coupon codes, no trickery involved. And some even list success rates. Try CouponAlbum.com, CouponCabin.com, CouponChief.com, CouponCodes4u.com, CouponCraze.com, CouponMountain.com, CouponSmarter.com, CouponWinner.com, CurrentCodes.com, GoGoShopper.com, IceTab.com, MyCoupons.com, NaughtyCodes.com, PromotionalCodes.com, RetailMeNot.com, SlickDeals.net, Tjoos.net, and a million others. Once you find a site you like and which seems to be the most comprehensive, add it to your Favorites. Trust me, you will not remember the name of it the next time you want to go there.

- You can check other rebate sites for coupon codes. Many of them just list the codes, while some are trickier and make you click on a link to get the code (then when you click on the link you have to sign in). I stick to the ones that list them outright. Here I'll list the same rebate sites I mentioned previously: BigCrumbs.com, eBates.com, ExtraBux.com, FatWallet.com, GreenBackStreet.com, MoreRebates.com, MrRebates.com, RebateShare.com, Spree.com, and there may be others.

There are occasions where using a coupon code found outside of the rebate site you are using will void your cash-back. The example which first comes to mind is Kohls.com. Kohl's generally has fantastic prices and coupon codes already listed, but there have been one or two occasions where there wasn't a suitable code at that moment. I searched and found a 15% off coupon elsewhere and decided since that was greater than the 3% cash-back, I would still use it.

Do not be discouraged if you can't find a coupon code. Generally, it's only the larger stores which offer codes, not the lesser known or new places. Don't use a coupon code just because it's fun; make sure you're still getting the best deal. If you can get a lower price on a different site without having to use a coupon code, there's nothing wrong with that! Sometimes, there just aren't any coupons available. It is very disappointing when that happens, but at some point you have to give up looking.

Precautions to Safeguard Your Internet Purchases

I've intermittently mentioned some red flags to watch out for but I'll go over them and add some more.

- If you've never heard of a website you're thinking about purchasing from, don't discard it, review it. On your search bar, type the store's website (i.e. Target.com) then the word "reviews." As far as the results you get, I think no news is good news. People don't write about the good experiences, just the bad. So if you can't find anything, *maybe* it means there's nothing bad with the service or products...??! If you do find some negative reviews, make a judgment call. Maybe you will still buy from the site as long as you don't find more than X number of negative reviews, or maybe you'll still buy as long you don't read anything about products falling apart. I can think of one site, in particular, that I read multiple bad reviews on. I still bought, because the prices were so outstanding I had to try and I ended up with no issues. Your call.

- You can also research the company. On the website itself, look for the link titled "About Us" or similar. Here, you might find information such as how long the company has been in business, where the company is established, etc. You might also try the "Contact Us" link and call the phone number listed. If you get a real person from the actual company, that's a great sign. If you get a busy tone or a number that has been disconnected then you might reconsider. Check out the Better Business Bureau, as well, at BBB.org. Do not simply trust the symbol on the seller's site; they can easily paste that as a picture without actually being a member.

- If there is only a dollar or two difference between a large, reputable company and a company you've never heard of, decide how much peace of mind is worth to you.

- Make sure you are totally aware of the return policy before buying. Numerous sites allow you to return items, but only if you pay the shipping to do so. Other's offer to pay the shipping, but only offer a refund within seven days. Then other stores such as Kohl's, Target, Wal-Mart, and other large retailers allow you to return items to the physical store, thus bypassing the shipping fee. Determine what you think is acceptable because at some point, you will have to return something.

- Whenever possible, make your purchase with PayPal or some other checkout site which does not show the seller your credit card information. Not only does this lesson the chance of your information being compromised, but those sites usually offer some sort of buyer protection policy,

- If PayPal or another anonymous method is not available, use a credit card. And I mean a real credit card, not your debit card ran as a credit card. Also, don't use e-check. There's nothing wrong with the processes themselves, but an actual credit card allows you to put a claim on that transaction before paying for it. If you use your debit card or an e-check, the money comes out of your account and if something goes wrong, you have to hope for a refund.

- If you are purchasing something of the electronic nature that plugs in (iPod, speakers, printer, refrigerator, etc.), you may want to strongly consider purchasing an extended warranty. But there are varied views on the subject of extended warranties and here's a light summary of general opinions:
  - ✓ Keep in mind that most electronics come with a warranty. If you bought a lemon, you usually know right away and it'll be covered under the original warranty.
  - ✓ Most electronics will last at least five years and your warranty will most likely run out before you have to use it.
  - ✓ If you have to mail the item out for service, consider the "hassle factor." It may be three months or more before you get your item back.
  - ✓ Make sure to read the fine print, as it's possible the damage you're most likely to encounter is considered "normal wear and tear" and therefore not covered.

- ✓ If the warranty costs more than the replacement of the item, reconsider.
- ✓ If the item is very expensive and would be hard to replace, the warranty might be a good idea.
- ✓ If you can return to the item to a storefront for service, that is a bonus.
- ✓ If the item is used (i.e. a floor model or refurbished) the original warranty might be non-existent and therefore an extended warranty might be justified.
- ✓ Visit SquareTrade.com if you are purchasing from eBay and would like to consider a warranty.
- ✓ Read your credit card agreements. American Express and some Visa cards extend the warranty for items purchased with that credit card.
- Whether or not you buy an extended warranty, always keep the receipt. If you bought the item on the internet, print out the confirmation page. I have a book of manuals for most of the items in my house and the receipts are stapled to them.
- It is worth your three minutes to fill out the product registration cards mailed with your item. This registration makes service faster and more efficient.

I have purchased items off the internet countless times, maybe thousands. I can say with confidence that chances are you will encounter no issues with 95% of your transactions. But I can also guarantee that as you buy more and more through cyberspace, you are bound to have some sort of problem. If you practice the aforementioned safeguards, you will lower the odds even further. For the troubles you do have, practice your patience (as claims through PayPal and credit card companies take up to a month or more) and remember you get more with honey than you do with vinegar.

Precautions for Buying on Craigslist

A lot of people don't buy on Craigslist because they think it's unsafe, and of course there are stories (true ones) out there. I don't claim to be a Craigslist expert, but I do have a few suggestions to help:

✓ If there aren't many pictures of an item or the pictures are fuzzy, email the seller asking for more pictures. That way, you can possibly decide against the item without going to see it.

✓ Don't be rushed into buying something. Yes, good items move fast but if you need more time to think about a purchase and the item moves, then just accept that it was meant to be. Maybe something better will come along.

✓ Do not give money to hold an item. Period.

✓ Always get the name and contact information for the seller.

✓ If you're going to a person's house to see an item, try to take someone along or, at the very least, let someone important know where you're going and give them the contact info.

✓ For small items, always try to meet in a public place, rather than someone's house. But don't let that make you feel obligated to purchase if you're unsure.

✓ If you're purchasing an item that plugs in, ALWAYS turn it on and use it before you buy.

✓ If you're purchasing an item that has batteries, only buy if you are able to test it out first.

✓ If you are receiving delivery for an item, don't pay for it until you receive and inspect it.

Always try to negotiate the price. Most sellers list their items knowing buyers are going to haggle. If they're firm, they're firm, but it's worth a try.

Good luck!

Chapter Six

eBay – Yes, It Gets Its Own Chapter

I almost put eBay in the "Shopping on the Internet" chapter but then decided to give it its own.

Most people I know don't shop on eBay because either they don't have the patience to find an object, don't have the patience to wait for the auction to end, don't want to take the "risk", or all of the above. In this chapter, I address all three of those issues! Give eBay a chance, and you stand to save a ton of money.

Finding Stuff on eBay

You might think that since there are billions of items up for sale on this site that finding the one you want is nearly impossible. Not so! Yes, there are billions of items for sale but the company is continuously changing their format (much to my irritation but I eventually get used to it and see the point) so as to make the site more user-friendly. If you're really motivated, you can click on "Help" on the upper right corner and go through a couple tutorials. But really, the key is to be specific, very specific.

First and foremost, I highly recommend doing the long-way search through the categories before typing anything. Why? Because there are so many sellers listing in so many different ways using so many different titles. Some are specific, some are vague, some have misspellings, and some leave out important words. But the one thing they have in common is they had to list within certain categories. My example: I was looking for a gift card for at least $50. I went to categories, gift certificates, then selected the one merchant I wanted. I was able to punch in a minimum amount. Then I saw the results, including one which was about to end yet the bids weren't very high. On closer inspection, there was nothing wrong with the item, but the seller didn't put the word "card" in his title. He had "gift certificate" but not "gift card." Most people who search don't go the long way; they just type what they want in the main screen. So when buyers punched in "gift card" as a search, this person's item didn't show up in the results. His loss, my gain, and I saved close to $30 (highly unusual for that store).

*Search the long way through Categories
for the best results and best deals*

eBay offers very user-friendly filter options

Of course you don't have to go the long way; sometimes you just want to type in your keywords. If you read the section on searching the internet where I discussed using quotation marks and minus signs, great! The same rules apply, only with a few extras I wish the search engines would employ. The following suggestions are good when searching titles of items:

- When you want a certain phrase, put quotations around the words. Now, in most circumstances, this won't really be necessary. But sometimes you get unexpected results in your search. For instance, let's say you're looking for Walking Wings, which is an invention by Upspring to help your baby learn to walk without killing your back. If you type Walking Wings without quotations, you will get some of the baby items, but also Red Wing Walking Shoes. So put the quotations on and you get only the baby results. (You would have avoided the shoes by going through the categories.)

- If you want something like blue jeans, I do not recommend putting quotations because you never know how someone is going to describe their item. One person will say "blue jeans" and another will say "size 8 jeans blue." Always try *no* quotations first. Better yet, just put "jeans." How many people actually call jeans "blue jeans"? Or, go the long route: Categories, Clothing, Men's/Women's Clothing, Jeans then select your size.

- If your search is flexible, utilize the parentheses. For example, you want a nightstand which is made out of wood or looks like it's made out of wood. You aren't too picky on the grain, you just don't want it to be a dark color. Try to think of several lighter shades of wood, as well of some other adjective, then search. Here's what mine would look like:

nightstand (natural, light, oak, honey, maple)

Your search results will all have the word "nightstand" but will only have one or two of the words from the parentheses. I get a little over 100 results, which honestly is an almost perfect number to sift through. Notice that I didn't put the word "wood" in my search! This is because only a small percentage of sellers would add that word; for the most part, they figure the word "maple" or "oak" implies wood and the title can only be so long. (If I include "wood," my results drop to about thirty and I could miss out on The One.)

• One of my favorite eBay search tools is the minus sign. I recently bought a flip flop sofa (not off of eBay, but I looked there). I didn't want any metal and I didn't want it to be white or black. My search looked like this:

(flip flop sofa, klik klak) –metal -white -black

I received thirteen results. Here's how that search translates to eBay:

Search using parentheses and utilize the sort options

✓ Search for the words flip, flop, *and* sofa OR klik *and* klak. I included "klik klak" because after some research, I realized different companies call this type of sofa by that name also).

✓ If any of those listings contain the words metal, white, *or* black, do not show it

- The minus sign is also helpful when you have a bunch of unwanted listings. For instance, Lowes the hardware store always has a ton of coupons floating around. While I know these are beneficial, there was one day I was only looking for a gift card. The frustrating thing for me was that sellers included these coupon listings in the same category as the gift cards (can't blame them, there's nowhere else to put them). So my search ended up like this: Lowe* -coupon* -percent –off. I'll explain the asterisk next... The minus sign let me omit the coupon listings with ease.

- Now, why the heck did I just type the asterisk? First, sellers spell the names of companies in many ways. There could be Lowes, Lowe's, Lowes', etc. I wanted to include all spelling variations so I put the asterisk after Lowe to tell eBay I wanted all listings that included a word that begins with "lowe". Second, if I typed "-coupon" I would still have listings with the word "coupons" returned. So I put the asterisk on to omit all listings that contain a word beginning with "coupon". I also use the asterisk when searching for Kohl's items (Kohl*).

- For a summary of these search tools, visit the reference chart in Chapter Seven.

If you utilize these search tips, your search experience will be much faster and efficient. Just have a little patience while you practice with them, and before you know it you'll be an eBay pro.

Can't Wait for the Auction to End?

Here's where I think the biggest deterrent is: the wait to win an item. Well, that's going to be a given in most instances, but there are two other ways to win and a couple different tools to employ to make your wait shorter.

1. *Buy It Now.* Sellers and eBay store owners have the option to set a Buy It Now price, which is the price they'll accept for the item and you can pay for the item immediately. Some items are up for auction with a Buy It Now price. If you are bidding on the auction, and someone comes along and pays the price, the auction ends and you lose the item. Other items aren't up for auction, they are just up for sale for that one price. If this Buy It Now route sounds like your type of cookie, then scroll down and on the left side of the screen until you see "Buying Formats" and you can select only items which offer a Buy It Now price.

2. *Best Offer.* If you think the Buy It Now price is too high or you'd like to score an even better deal, see if the seller has added the "Best Offer" option to their item. This route is not as immediate as the Buy It Now, as you have to wait for the seller to respond and they are allowed to receive multiple offers. Keep in mind, if the seller accepts your offer, you are then

bound to the eBay "contract" and required to purchase the item.

3. *Ending Soonest.* This is actually my preferred method,
   as I think auction-style listings are generally cheaper
   than Buy It Now. So when the results from my search
   show up, I often organize them by "Ending Soonest."
   You'll see items that are ending in several minutes
   increasing to newly listed items. If I see one that is
   ending within ten to twenty minutes and is within a
   reasonable price, I try to be that shark that comes in
   the last two minutes to steal the item from the current top bidder. People like me can be so infuriating!
   But we also get the best deals...
4. *Max Bid.* If you are willing to wait for the auction to
   end but don't feel like bidding a million times, there
   is the option to set a "Max Bid." I love this feature; I
   put in the highest price I am willing to pay and then
   wait till I get an email saying I either won the item
   or I didn't.

Here's a tip on how to win items for less: find auctions ending on a weekday, not a weekend. Most buyers
are browsing on their days off- Saturday and more likely
Sunday. More buyers means more bids which means
higher prices. Shop during the week and you'll have less
competition! (The reverse goes for selling. If you're selling an item, you want your auction to end on a Sunday
evening.) Please bear in mind that I give you those tips
based solely on my experience, not due to some statistical
research.

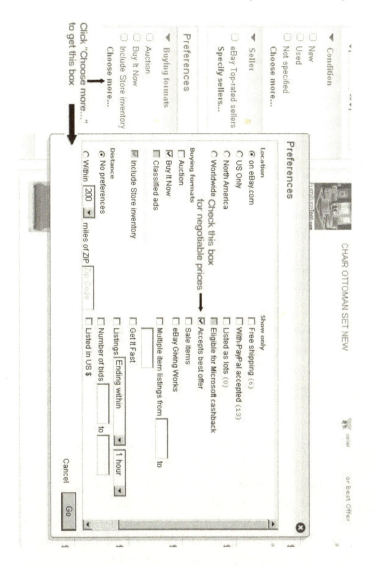

How to see only Buy It Now or Best Offer items

Isn't buying from people on eBay risky?

In a word, yes. But eBay and PayPal have put in place some great methods to make your shopping experience safer. If you follow these guidelines (again, based only on my practice) then you can help prevent problems from occurring in the first place:

1. Don't buy from sellers with a feedback rating of less than fifty. Adjust that number according to the price of the item. What do I mean? When I bought our appliances on eBay (yes, I really did and they turned out awesome!) I made sure the seller had an adequate number of feedbacks (over 1000) and a very high rating (over 99%). When I purchase a book for fifty cents, I'm willing to go with the newbies. The reason this works is because eBay does not allow repeatedly offending sellers to continue their business, but also higher feedback means more eBay experience. That counts for a lot, as you'll discover once you get going.

2. If you're buying something electronic, make sure the seller offers a return policy. Electronics can be finicky and you just may get a lemon. If there's no return policy, you're out of luck and out of money.

3. Fully understand the return policy, if there is one. Many sellers require the buyer to pay shipping for the return of an item, which we all know can be pricey! If the item is huge and/or heavy, it may not be worth your time or money to return it. For every purchase, ask yourself what you would do if the item were "faulty." This is why, for some purchases, I have

decided to go with an actual company like Amazon, as they provide paid UPS pick-up of returned items.

4. Completely read the listing! Boy this is important. And I'm still my own victim on this! Recently, my husband needed white pants so I went on eBay and bought some. When Rob saw them he said, "These aren't white!" and he was right, they were like a cream color. Of course, I was immediately mad at the seller and went online to complain. Well, the listing actually says, "Soft White" and they don't offer a return policy. So guess who's stuck with cream pants?

5. Ask questions before bidding. If you don't completely understand the listing or the listing is missing some vital details, use the link to ask the seller a question. Sure, this can be tedious but it's well worth it, trust me. And if the seller doesn't respond, don't buy the item!

6. Only, only, only use PayPal. Never, ever send a check or money order. And make sure the seller accepts PayPal! I'd venture to say that most do, but there's that 1% that doesn't- often, their items go for very cheap (because no one wants to take the risk) so if you see an item for an ultra-low price, ask yourself "Why?"

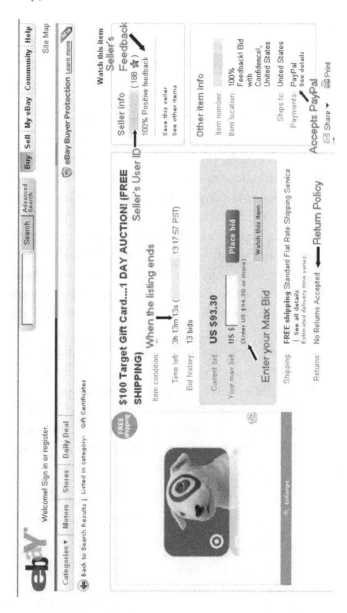

A summary of how to read the listing details

Please please please...

Leave feedback! Good sellers rely on their feedback ratings to earn and sustain buyers' trust. Good buyers rely on their feedback ratings to be eligible for large purchases and to boost their ego. So whether you're buying or selling, please always leave feedback to maintain this system! Remember, though, many sellers do not leave feedback until the buyer does so for them.

To Recap: the Dos and Don'ts

DO:
- Shop through your rebate site
- Be specific when searching to find the exact item you're looking for
- Search through categories (the long way) to find the best deals
- Utilize quotation marks, minus signs, parentheses, and asterisks in your search
- Specifically search for Buy It Now and Best Offer listings if you want an item soon
- Arrange your results by Ending Soonest to find auctions which are close to ending
- Put in your Max Bid so you can "set it and forget it"
- Weed out sellers with low feedback numbers for important and/or pricey items
- Be open to new sellers when it comes to "safer" items, like books
- Look for a return policy and fully understand it
- Read the listing in entirety and ask questions if something's not clear
- Assure PayPal is accepted

- Only pay with PayPal
- Leave feedback!!!

DON'T:
- Get frustrated if your search yields 10,000 results. Just be more specific...
- Just pay the Buy It Now price if a Best Offer option is listed
- Forget to employ the search filters and arrangements (i.e. Price: low to high)
- Go with a new seller if the item is very expensive
- Assume anything about the listing! Always ask questions if you're uncertain
- Pay with cash, check or money order

The Hidden eBay Goldmine

I know I previously mentioned buying gift cards on eBay and the internet but I'm going to emphasize it here now. Do a search on eBay: go to "Categories" then "Gift Certificates" and you will see the obscene number of gift cards that are for sale! Most are in auction format but there are plenty Buy It Now items, too. eBay makes it easy to search for your particular merchant or type or price.

Let's say you buy a $100 for $92, including shipping. Alright, you saved $8, right off the bat. But if you went through your rebate site like you always do, then you also received a 3% cash-back rebate, putting your net payment as $89.24 if I did my math correctly. So you saved over $10!! In general, the higher the gift card balance, the more you'll save. Under $50, you can expect to save between one and five dollars. Over $250 and you can save between $15 and $30!

Another savings route I like to take is coupons. There aren't that many food items on eBay but there are plenty of coupons! There are people who make their living by clipping coupons and selling them on eBay, believe it or not. Recently I bought fifteen coupons for this one juice I like, all valued at $0.75 each- I paid $1.40, including shipping. I did, actually, use all fifteen so I saved over $9. If you are lucky enough to be able to buy and store in bulk, think about looking for coupons on eBay!

If you take the time to "get to know" eBay, you stand to save a lot of money!

Chapter Seven

Reference Charts

Where to Buy on the Internet

Item	Websites to Check Out
Airline Tickets	Pick your favorite airline and add .com
Books (Non-Textbook)	Amazon.com, AbeBooks.com, Alibris.com, Biblio.com, BookCloseouts.com, BookFinder.com, DiscountNewAndUsedBooks.com, eBay.com, Half.com
Car Rentals	CarRentalExpress.com, CarRentals.com, E-ZRentACar.com, RentACar.com, RentalCarMomma.com, RentalCars.com, USave.com, VroomVroomVroom.com plus sites listed under "Vacations"
Cell Phone	LetsTalk.com, Wirefly.com

Item	Websites to Check Out
Clothing and Shoes	15DollarStore.com, 599Fashion.com, 6pm.com, BlueFly.com, DSW.com, Kohls.com, ModaXpressOnline.com, ShoeBuy.com, ShoeSteal.com, Zappos.com, plus a million others...
Cleaning Supplies-Organic	Drugstore.com, MrsMeyers.com, PlanetNatural.com, SeventhGeneration.com, Vitacost.com
Eating out	Restaurant.com, ValPak.com, or try the discount gift cards
Electronics	Amazon.com, BestBuy.com, Buy.com, CircuitCity.com, Crutchfield.com, eBay.com, Frys.com, JR.com, Overstock.com, RadioShack.com, Target.com, TigerDirect.com, Walmart.com
Food – Organic/Special Diet	Amazon.com, HealthSuperstore.com, LuckyVitamin.com, NaturalGrocers.com, OrganicDirect.com, ShopOrganic.com, TheBetterHealthStore.com, TrueFoodsMarket.com, Vitacost.com

Item	Websites to Check Out
Furniture	Craigslist.com, DirectlyHome.com, eBay.com, Furniture.com, FurnitureDealDirect.com, FurnitureESuperstore.com, FurnitureOnTheWeb.com, Overstock.com, RoomsToGo.com, RoomStore.com, TheFurnitureWarehouse.net
Gas	FuelEconomy.gov, GasBuddy.com, GasPrices.MapQuest.com, GasPriceWatch.com, MotorTrend.com
Gift Cards	ABCGiftCards.com, CityDeals.com, eBay.com, GiftCardRescue.com, GiftCards4Less.com, GiftCardsAgain.com, GiftCardSwapping.com, MonsterGiftCard.com, PlasticJungle.com, StarGiftCardExchange.com, SwapAGift.com, etc.
Health Products	Amazon.com, CVS.com, Drugstore.com, eBay.com, GNC.com, HealthSuperstore.com, HealthWarehouse.com, LuckyVitamin.com, Puritan.com, QVC.com, RiteAid.com, Vitacost.com, VitaminShoppe.com, Walgreens.com

Item	Websites to Check Out
Hotels	Booking.com, Hotel.info, HotelReservation.com, Hotels.com, QuickBook.com, Otel.com, RoomSaver.com plus sites listed under "Vacations"
Landscaping & Gardening	BloomingBulb.com, Brecks.com, Garderners.com, GardensAlive.com, Gurneys.com, HenryFields.com, SpringHillNursery.com, TastefulGarden.com
Magazines	BestDealMagazines.com, BlueDolphin.com, DiscountMagazines.com, DiscountMags.com, eMagazines.com, Magazines.com, MagMall.com, ValueMags.com
Movie rentals	For physical locations: RedBox.com or MovieCube.com. For online: Blockbuster.com or Netflix.com
Newspapers	DiscountedNewspapers.com
Personal Hygiene - Expensive	Amazon.com, Avon.com, CVS.com, Drugstore.com, eBay.com, HealthWarehouse.com, Kohls.com, LuckyVitamin.com, Overstock.com, Puritan.com, QVC.com, RiteAid.com, ShopNBC.com, SkinStore.com, Target.com, Vitacost.com, VitaminShoppe.com, Walgreens.com, Walmart.com

Item	Websites to Check Out
Pet supplements and smaller items	1800PetMeds.com, Amazon.com, DrsFosterSmith.com, eBay.com, EntirelyPets.com, Medi-Vet.com, PetCo.com, Petsmart.com
Textbooks	Amazon.com, BigWords.com, CampusBooks.com, CheapestTextbooks.com, eBay.com, eCampus.com, Half.com, Textbooks.com. For textbook rental: Chegg.com
Vacations	BestFares.com, Expedia.com, Hotwire.com, Kayak.com, LowFares.com, Orbitz.com, Priceline.com, SideStep.com, Travelocity.com, TravelZoo.com, TripAdvisor.com

To Buy on the Internet or
Not To Buy on the Internet?

Item	Buy on the Internet?	Buy at the Store?	Explanation or Examples
Books and magazines	Yes	No	Internet, internet, internet.
Candles, picture frames, trinkets, etc.	No	Yes	You can find these items on the internet but you'll spend hours and won't save that much money.
Cell Phone	Yes	No	There are so many more offers and deals than what you'll find in the store.
Cleaning supplies	No	Yes	For the solutions, shipping costs are high. The tools (i.e. sponges) are generally inexpensive and not worth paying any shipping cost.
Clothing and shoes	Yes	Yes	Clearance racks!!! For stores: Kohl's, Ross, Marshall's, T.J. Maxx, Plato's Closet, Goodwill. For bulk lots or expensive items, search the internet.

Item	Buy on the Internet?	Buy at the Store?	Explanation or Examples
Eating out	Yes	Yes	Know when your favorite restaurants have specials. Buy discounted gift certificates at Restaurant.com. Look for coupons in ValPak, phone book, newspaper, mailings, etc.
Electronics	Yes	Yes	If buying online, it's safer (in my opinion) to stick with well-known stores.
Food	No	Yes	Exception: organic or special diet items (buy those on the internet if you can)
Furniture	Yes	Yes	Stores: outlet or second-hand. Internet: try Craigslist first!
Gift Cards	Yes	No	At least try the swap sites first...
Health Products	Yes	No	You'll save tons via the internet!

Item	Buy on the Internet?	Buy at the Store?	Explanation or Examples
Landscaping & Gardening	Yes	Yes	Buy soil, mulch, bricks, etc. at the stores. Buy bulbs and plants online, if you can wait for them!
Movie rentals	Yes	Yes	For physical locations: RedBox.com or MovieCube.com. For online: Blockbuster.com or Netflix.com.
Personal Hygiene - Inexpensive	No	Yes	Shampoo, lotion, toothpaste, deodorant, etc. Exception: organic products (buy on internet)
Personal Hygiene - Expensive	Yes	No	Razor blades, perfume/cologne, wrinkle cream, etc.
Pet food and litter	No	Yes	Shipping costs will bite you due to weight! Better stick with the stores...
Pet supplements and smaller items	Yes	No	Just like human supplements, physical stores charge way more than internet stores.

Item	Buy on the Internet?	Buy at the Store?	Explanation or Examples
Textbooks	Yes	No	If you don't at least try to buy these on the internet, you're crazy!

Internet Search Tools

Tool	Purpose	Use for search engine?	Use for eBay?
Quotations	Search for EXACT phrase *Example: "area rug"*	Yes	Yes
Minus Sign	Exclude certain words from results *Example: -black –white -metal*	Yes	Yes
OR	Search for a variety of words *Example: maple OR pine OR oak*	Yes	No
Parenthesis	Search for a variety of words, equivalent to OR *Example: (black, white, brown)*	No	Yes
Asterisk (search engine)	Wildcard to fill in the blank *Example: world's population * people*	Yes	No
Asterisk (eBay)	Search for variations of a word *Example: lowe* (will return lowe, lowes, lowe's, lowest, etc.)*	No	Yes
Asterisk with Minus Sign (eBay)	Exclude variations of a word *Example: -coupon* (will exclude coupon, coupons, etc.)*	No	Yes

Happy

Shopping!

About the Author

Cristy Johnson resides in a very modest home in Durham, NC. She is accompanied by her husband and young son, with another baby on the way. Her two cats also share her home, which she much appreciates.

www.ingramcontent.com/pod-product-compliance
Lightning Source LLC
Chambersburg PA
CBHW051246050326
40689CB00007B/1091